Defending The Faith
In The Last Days:
A Transforming Christian
Worldview of Religion,
Philosophy, and Science

By Dr. John G. Leslie

Deluge Press

The fear of the Lord is the beginning of knowledge: but a fool despises wisdom and instruction. Proverbs 1:7

For the Word of God is living and active and sharper than any two-edged sword, and piercing as far as the division of soul and spirit, of both joints and marrow, and able to judge the thoughts and intents of the heart. Hebrews 4:12

DEDICATION

To my dear wife Barbara, a woman of God according to Proverbs 31, and my children who are serving God according to Proverbs 22:6.

DEFENDING THE FAITH IN THE LAST DAYS:
A TRANSFORMING CHRISTIAN WORLDVIEW
OF RELIGION, PHILOSOPHY AND SCIENCE

CONTENTS

	Acknowledgments	i
	Introduction	1
1	The Inter-relationships of Religion, Philosophy and Science	3
2	Religion	9
3	Philosophy	45
4	Science	75
5	Conclusion	95
	What must I do to be saved?	103
	Why I Believe in God and not Evolution	104
	Selected Bibliography	107
	About the Author	111

ACKNOWLEDGMENTS

Many people have helped me in the development of the thoughts contained in these pages. Not all would agree with what I have written, and any errors or misperceptions remain my own.

I give thanks to parents who loved me, Doris and John C. Leslie, and gratitude to a brother, Greg, and sisters Nancy and Jennifer, who have encouraged me. I appreciate the support of Clarice Leslie, Buddy and Lorraine Fisher, and Dr. and Mrs. Paul Fisher.

Many teachers have influenced me: Dr. Lawrence Sandberg, Dr. Barry Oakes, Dr. Durwood Ray (and other ORU professors), Dr. Henry Morris, Dr. Clifford Wilson and Dr. Steven Collins.

Christian ministers and teachers include Ken Ham, Richard Exley, John Luginbuhl, Roger Scarbro, Brian Thewlis, Jim Powers, and Greg Johnson. Others include Jim Brown, and Herb Moser, who kindly reviewed this text.

My family including my wife Barbara, and my children, Peter, Anna, and Teresa, continue to be a blessing to me.

INTRODUCTION

The Biblical scriptures say, "Be diligent to present yourself approved to God as a workman who does not need to be ashamed, handling accurately the word of truth," and "always being ready to make a defense to everyone who asks you to give an account for the hope that is in you," (2 Timothy 2:15; 1 Peter 3:15). Elsewhere it says that we should be wise as serpents and innocent as doves, discerning the times, and not taken captive by the vain philosophies of men (Matthew 10:16, Matthew 16:3, Colossians 2:8). Our age is the Informational Age. Yet this book contends that much of the information being purveyed is not God honoring nor true to Biblical principles. This is seen in the dichotomy that while a majority of American adults believe in God, 60-70% do not believe in absolute truth. The inconsistency has been passed on to the youth. Seventy-five percent of young adults, 18-34 years old, believe in relative ethics. Other surveys of the 12-19 year old males and females reveal similar trends. Americans lack an understanding of who God is.

This book reviews the areas of religion, philosophy, and science. Their inter-relationship profoundly affects one's perspective of life. The common religions and philosophies of the ages along with the development and uses of science are discussed and compared with and often contrasted to Christian principles. It is believed that the Christian, by having knowledge of the Scriptures and a cursory knowledge of secular views, will be more able to defend their faith and assist in converting the sinner. The text is written as a concise resource to be used by the busy parents for instructing high school teens, for assistance in introductory studies for the college age student, and for any other interested person. By it, may the reader continue to grow in their knowledge and grace of the Lord Jesus Christ.

CHAPTER 1

THE INTER-RELATIONSHPS OF RELIGION, PHILOSOPHY, AND SCIENCE

It is the glory of God to conceal a matter and the privilege of man to seek it out. Yet, God has promised this to those who seek Him; His Spirit will guide them (Proverbs 25:2, John 14:17). The purpose of man on this earth is to first be converted from self will to God's will, from the kingdom of darkness to that of light. When a man confesses Jesus Christ as Lord and accepts His teachings, this conversion results in the free gift of regeneration of the spirit of man; also described as being "born again". The believer is then to imitate Christ, and be formed into the image of Christ. In this process the mind is to be renewed to God's word, the emotions remolded, and the will disciplined. The sensations of the body are to be subjected to healthy behavior. Thus, God wants to impact man's entire being: spirit, soul, and body. As man puts on Christ, he or she becomes an ambassador for Him and others become converted; that is, they turn from their own ways, to Him. This is the ultimate will of God in this current age. This is the glory of God hidden: eternal life and fellowship with Him, revealed to those who respond to Him.

It is essential for Christian growth and vitality that the believer in Jesus Christ understands that he has a spirit, soul, and body (Hebrews 4:12; 1 Thessalonians 5:23). The Bible describes man as the temple or tabernacle of God (John 2:21; 2 Corinthians 6:16). God, through the use of the structure of the tabernacle instructs man about the ministry of the Messiah, Jesus Christ, and also the character and function of the triune nature of man. The Outer Court corresponds to man's body, the Holy Place to the soul, and the Holy of Holies to the residence of the spirit (**see Figure 1**- God's Tabernacle and The Tabernacle of Man).

FIGURE 1

God's Tabernacle

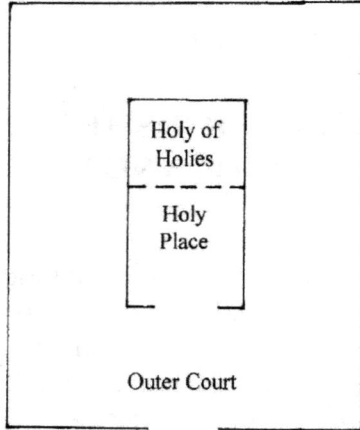

The Tabernacle of Man

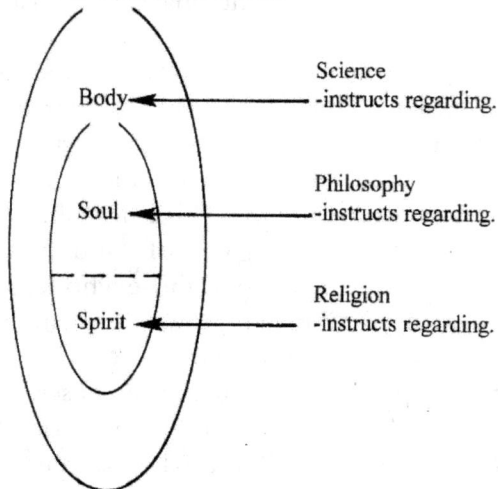

The body is simply the physical life and vehicle of man in this present age. Watchman Nee (a Chinese Christian writer) elucidates the function of the soul as volition, mind, and emotion; and the spirit (of man) as composed of conscience, intuition, and communion with God's Spirit, if the person is "born again." Reverend Clarence Larkin has commented on man's condition before and after being "born again." He says, "In his un-fallen state the 'spirit' of man was illuminated from Heaven, but when the human race fell in Adam, sin closed the window of the spirit, and pulled down the curtain (between the Holy Place and the Holies of Holies), and the 'chamber of the spirit' became a Death Chamber, and remains so in every unregenerate heart, until the 'life' and 'light' giving power of the Holy Spirit floods that chamber with the 'life' and 'light' giving power of the new life in Christ Jesus. We see then why the 'natural' man cannot understand spiritual things. He cannot understand them until his spiritual nature has been renewed." Without God, the unregenerate man becomes soul, rather than spirit dominated.

In man's fallen state, God initially appeals to him through the mind, i.e. sense and reasoning. That is, He uses the creation to reveal His general attributes to mankind (Romans 1:18-21), and His Spirit deals directly with them regarding the issues of sin, righteousness, and judgment.

As theologian Charles Ryrie comments on John 16:8, "The Spirit, through the apostles, evangelists, and preachers, will convict the world. To convict means to set forth the truth of the gospel in such clear light that men are able to accept or reject it intelligently..." If a person, after hearing the gospel and being "moved" upon by God's Spirit yields himself to God, God will then fellowship with and infuse that man's spirit. The man becomes "born again". God then promises to reveal Himself directly to the man, as a Father to a son or a daughter (Romans 8:15,16). Regenerate man is taught spiritual things, and thus begins the maturation process of bringing man's spirit into dominion over his soul and body (as it was before the fall). Watchman Nee warns Christians not to seek to acquire knowledge alone, for this is the temptation that Eve and Adam fell into: eating the fruit of the knowledge of good and evil, apart from God's presence and guidance. In this they allowed their souls to gain dominance over their spirits. Rather knowledge should be prayerfully sought, allowing the Spirit of God to help the believer place it in the right context, holding onto that which is good.

Because man is a triune being, spirit, soul, and body, God uses religion, philosophy, and science to reveal himself to man and to help man understand the true nature of God and mankind. From this each individual develops his/her worldview of life.

Science, the observations of nature, is assessed through the five senses. It gives man examples of God's power; "truth springs forth from the earth" (Psalm 85:11), and "the heavens declare the glory of God" (Psalm 19:11). By science, technology is developed to subdue the earth. Yet, both man and the physical realm are corrupted, for "all of the creation groans, waiting for its redemption" (Romans 8:19-23).

It is only through a Biblical understanding that Christians know the earth is not as it was originally created. It has both the handiwork of the Creator and the marks of sin in it. For example, the Bible describes the times before the sin of Adam, and after the return of Christ, when sickness does not exist. Secular man lacks or rejects this knowledge and attempts to explain nature by its present condition. Yet how does one comprehend the concepts of holiness, purity in a naturalistic setting?

Sin, the willful disobedience to God's will and word, has resulted in physical pain and sufferings (Genesis 3:14-19). The human body has become influenced by unnatural cravings. Man reaps in his body the choices he makes, e.g. sexually transmitted diseases from immoral relations; lung cancer from smoking, etc. While science has helped relieve suffering, it will never eradicate it. Each Christian should understand basic health issues, and use their physical body as a vehicle for doing God's will in the earth. They can understand and use technology as well to help others to experience God's goodness. But the body is only one aspect of our being.

With philosophy mankind reasons. It is an activity of the mind and thus the soul. By it he deals with aspects of morals, conduct, and values. Secular man is dominated primarily by his mind. He reasons within a corrupt set of principles or worldviews. Thus his philosophies, while appearing wise, are not. For example, it was the downfall of David Hume, the Naturalists, and others (see Chapter 3, Philosophy) to assume that the physical realm is all that exists. As will be shown, by defining reality as only the physical realm, he and others excluded, by definition, the spirit and the soul without actually demonstrating their nonexistence. Thus, these writers were either ignorant or disingenuous regarding the impact of philosophic and religious concepts in their lives. Other secular philosophers such as Rousseau exalted soul centered reason and sensuality, which became their reality. This imbalance has led to great wars and bloodshed including the French Revolution, because man sought to "please the flesh", and lived by "survival of the fittest", and "did what was right in his own eyes". All of these philosophers inevitably chose to reject God's revealed will, especially the concept of sin and judgment. Each set up their own paradigms of reality and tended to define God within their system. In actuality, they often attempted to become a god and to seek followers; this was Satan's initial sin.

The Christian uses reason to understand God's principles: study to show yourself approved to God. As he gains a grasp of God's word he begins to understand the degree of impact sin has had on the creation, what motivates men and women, right and wrong behavior, and the reasonableness of judgment and eternal consequences. To the Christian, reason is a powerful tool with which to understand God. Yet the warning stands: "See to it that no one takes you captive through philosophy and empty deception according to the tradition of men," (Colossians 2:8).

Philosophy, including the use of reason, has a profound effect upon the wills of men. It can lead to great achievements or regrettable actions. The Christian must balance his reason by the guidance and rule of his spirit in communion with God's Spirit.

Religion is that system of core values upon which one trusts. It can include or exclude God. The secular (atheistic) philosopher and naturalistic scientist deny or minimize the spirit realm and God. Thus to them religion is by definition nonexistent or a construct set up by man. These people do man a great disservice, and they become the blind leading the blind.

Spiritualism or spiritism, the belief in a spirit dimension, is common but often followers perceive it contrary to Biblical principles. This is revealed in many contemporary movies. They reflect a belief in supernatural evil forces; but they have no examples of a living, holy God. Others attempt to explain the supernatural in naturalistic terms alone. Many religions reduce God to a being confined to their own physical universe or to one having fallen attributes like man. Thus, these have a form of religion but deny or lack an understanding of its real power (see 2 Timothy 3:5). They often disregard the observations of science and disdain philosophy yet partake of both. This has often led people into deep darkness; from child sacrifice to appeasing gods to the worship of Satan in hope of extracting some greater powers.

The Judeo-Christian scriptures alone give a correct view of the spirit realm. There are real demons; yet by faith in Christ, Christians do not need to fear them. God's Spirit does speak to men's spirits, contrary to Dr. Freud and others. By repentance man can have the spiritual weight of sin forgiven.

The Christian faith is not a blind faith. In fact, it is a faith of light founded on sound principles of reason/logic (but not worldly logic; see 1 Corinthians 1:18-2:16 and 1 Corinthians 3:18-21), observation, and conscience. As individuals mature as Christians they are being formed spirit, soul (mind), and body into Christ's likeness. This is God's glory in man (John 17). By this, Christians can give others a reason for the hope that lies within.

The next three chapters review religion, philosophy, and science. By gaining a correct perception of each, Christians may better comprehend God's will and His plan for mankind. They become more able to discern true from false beliefs. Each Christian is to then become an "ambassador for Christ, as though God were entreating through us; we beg you on behalf of Christ, be reconciled to God," (2 Corinthians 5:20). In Chapter 5 the conclusion of the characteristics and interfacing of the spirit (religion), soul (philosophy), and body (science) are reviewed. Recommendations of how to mature into the image of Christ in all three dimensions are given.

CHAPTER 2

RELIGION

Religion answers questions that no other domain of inquiry can answer. It answers what is unanswerable by any other means. As a dialogue written in 1826 stated,

> "Is there a heaven? Is there a hell? How shall I reach the one? How shall I reach the other? Let reason pronounce: let reason determine. It cannot. No created intelligence can come forward and satisfy me. Who can find out God, and his infinite mind and will? But look ye, companions; to be left in ignorance, or even doubt, on these things, is to be left without the first elements of religion ..."

Neither science nor philosophy, as will be shown, can answer whether there is heaven or hell. The answers to questions regarding absolute beginnings and ends must come from revelations outside of human experience. Thus religion should include the concept of an intelligent being greater than ourselves, i.e., God. However, in practice God is not always included in some definitions of religion.

Religion implies that which one relies on or is devoted to. If a person believes in God, then religion is associated with God, but to an atheist or agnostic, religion is a belief system that purposefully excludes the idea of God. In a broader sense, religion is the core set of principles upon which any individual depends, and thus it overlaps with their philosophy of life (discussed later). Each person should be able to sit down and give at least 5 to 10 principles that guide their life. From these, corollaries or subsets should follow. For example, a Christian believes:

1) God made the heavens and the earth.
2) Man was made in God's image but sinned (rebelled against Him).
3) Christ died for each person's sins.

4) Each person can through Christ be forgiven and thus,

5) Have eternal life with God.

These are core principles. From these follow corollaries such as: "Thou shall not steal, shall not bear false witness, covet your neighbor's property" etc. A belief in God is primary, therefore what He commands the Christian should obey.

For the atheist, by definition life must have arisen without being planned (i.e., no Creator), if he holds a concept of sin it must be relative to what he considers right and wrong (because he is judge), and if he holds to a concept of eternal life (which most don't), it must be due to an inherent, or unknown physical property of the universe. He can hold to similar corollaries as the Christian. e.g., don't steal, don't lie, don't lust after a neighbor's things, but he holds to this for completely different reasons. For example, some have said they accept a sort of non-theistic Ten Commandments because it is good for propagation of the human species.

The problem with being an atheist or agnostic is that everything becomes relative; right is whatever is correct in one's own eyes, or as a collective group. In this situation secular philosophic views become the dominant religious ones. Also, once one is committed to the position of an atheist he has closed his mind to evidence that may be supportive of a creator, and the opposite is not necessarily true. That is, a believer in God does not have to exclude evidence, in that no one is all knowing but the creator. The atheist by his position is <u>less impartial</u> than the believer in God and this will affect his/her approach to science as well (see Chapter 3 Philosophy and Chapter 4 Science). Yet, each does develop biases.

There comes a time when every Christian should develop a cursory understanding of the main religions of the world; not when a young believer, but when he or she has been rooted in Biblical principles. We are to be "shrewd as serpents and innocent as doves" (Matthew 10:16). We are to know something about others so as to "become all things to all men" and "be able to give reasons for the hope that lies within." Yet we are not to partake of their ways, but we are to confidently lift Jesus Christ up as the answer to the very deep needs of every human life. Parents should begin addressing these issues before a child leaves the home for he or she will encounter them afterwards. Christ is the greatest and final revelation of God and each Christian should know what makes Him so.

In the following sections the major religions are reviewed in outline form by Background and Tenets. Each one is then contrasted with Christian teachings; and approaches to evangelism of each of the groups are discussed. The list includes only the major faiths. Christianity, Judaism, and Islam are monotheistic religions. Hinduism is largely polytheistic. Finally, Confucius (not discussed), Buddhism, and Humanism are largely agnostic/atheistic. (Cults and occult groups make up a large but heterogeneous group.) Examples from each group are reviewed; from atheistic, cultic/occultic, polytheistic to monotheistic.

Approximate percentages of adherents to each faith are indicated below in **Figure 2** - this reveals a tremendous need for Christian evangelism of the peoples of the earth. A minimum of sixty-two percent of the world's people do not know the God of Abraham, Isaac, and Jacob as their Father and Jesus Christ as their Savior. In fact, numerous countries prohibit the teachings of Christianity and persecute believers. These include 1) Middle East - Saudi Arabia, Pakistan, Iran, Egypt; 2) Africa - Sudan, Nigeria; 3) East Asia - North Korea, China, Vietnam; and 4) South America - Columbia, Peru.

FIGURE 2

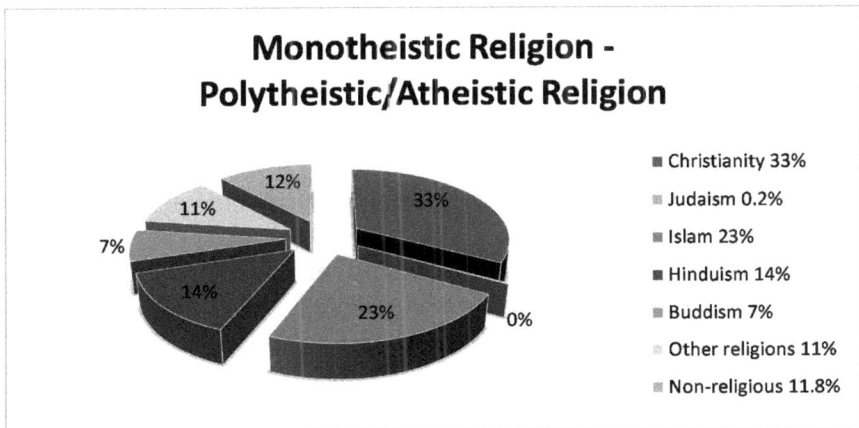

Monotheistic Religion - Polytheistic/Atheistic Religion

- Christianity 33%
- Judaism 0.2%
- Islam 23%
- Hinduism 14%
- Buddism 7%
- Other religions 11%
- Non-religious 11.8%

Humanism

Background

A membership brochure for a San Diego humanist group states, "Humanism is the belief that man shapes his own destiny. It is a non-theistic religion, a way of life...." The humanist believes knowledge, understanding and wisdom can be obtained apart from God , and that man, not God, is the ultimate judge. As Henry Morris documents in his book, The Long War Against God, some of mankind have been denying the existence of God since the Fall of Creation. Many men from earliest times have accepted only "naturalistic" (i.e., physical) explanations for the origin .and subsequent development of life. As will be discussed later, their religion is dominated by their philosophy. Democritus (406 BC), and Anaximander (610 BC) both propounded matter as the only reality, and the Great Chain of Being (non-theistic evolution) has been advocated from the earliest time through the Greek Atomists, Roman Lucretius, Darwin and Spencer to present advocates like S.J. Gould. As Gould has stated, "Why should the laymen be interested in so esoteric a subject as evolutionary biology? ... Because it tells us where we came from, how we got here, and perhaps where we are going. Quite simply, it is science's version of Roots, except it is the story of us all."

Well known humanists have included John Dewey, Bertrand Russell, Julian Huxley, Eric Fromm, and Isaac Asimov.

Tenets (based on the American Humanist Association-1933)
1) Universe self existent not created.
2) No supernatural.
3) "Man is a part of nature, and that he emerged as the result of a continuous process."
4) Man is to "rely on himself and his own powers" not the guidance of any supernatural being(s).
5) There are no final causes or purposes to life.
6) Society should be socialized into one economic order, "shared life in a shared world."

Christian Teachings/ Approaches to Evangelism

1) The concept of a Creator is central to any further concepts of God. Romans 1:20 tells us that God's eternal power, divine attributes, and invisible attributes are clearly displayed in the natural world to all men. It also says men suppress this knowledge. As man rejects God's witness to him, he enters a spiraling decadence (Romans 1:21-32). First they do not honor God and their speculations become darkened. They then, in false wisdom, begin to worship (study, exalt) nature i.e., naturalism (see Chapter 3 Philosophy). Next they begin to yield to the fleshly impulses - fornication, drug use, etc. This then devolves into homosexuality/ lesbianism, and the resultant diseases of such unions. They become wicked, envious of others, slanderers, hating God, unloving-all fruits of the flesh rather than the spirit (Galatians 5:19-21). The culmination is that they then rejoice in others doing the same. This leads to God's judgment-both for individuals and communities.

Lest a Christian become prideful; we have all been in that spiral of decadence, "for all have sinned and fall short of the glory of God" (Romans 3:23). So we know that God can, as a man responds to Him, pull man out of the spiral. Therefore, we should pray for, share with, and have expectant hope of God's intervention in others' lives, including humanists.

2) The humanist is extremely prideful. That is a tenet of his faith: that man is the ruler, the problem solver. He believes knowledge, understanding and wisdom can be obtained apart from God, which was the tool used by Satan against mankind in the Garden of Eden. Intellectual debating is often not fruitful, but in the workplace a consistent skilled work attitude and a kind heart can often turn one back to God. The humanist already has knowledge of God. According to the Bible, what they need is a real live example of Him working in the life of another person.

3) The humanist clearly has an agenda to turn all of society to his way of thinking. John Dewey has had a profound impact on the education system in America, Karl Marx in socialist governments, and even Wellhausen in theology (see Chapter 3 Philosophy). They specifically target the children of society. That is one reason why teaching evolution (the paradigm or world view used to justify humanism) in schools is so important to the humanist. One only has to look at the former Soviet Union and other socialist states to see

the results.

What is the Christian response to this?
1) Preach God's word in integrity.
2) Vote for leaders, and laws that support Christian principles.
3) Obey God's word and suffer the effects of an ungodly society with a pure heart and expectant hope in God Almighty.
4) Pray.

Buddhism (Vedic)

Background

Gautama Buddha was born in approximately 566 BC in northern India. His teachings were not recorded for nearly 500 years after his death. Lore has it that seeing apparent contradiction in his life and that of others he abandoned his life as a nobleman/husband and began wandering and searching for truth. He became "enlightened" while praying under a bo tree (tree of wisdom). R.A. Gard defines Buddhism as "a historical expression of a universal ideal. A voluntary way of thought and conduct, based upon an analysis of conditioned existence, dependent upon supreme human effort and directed toward the realization of freedom in perfect existence," - a religio-philosophic system.

Tenets

1) Truth of suffering: existence is pain, nothing is permanent, everything is in a cycle of stagnation, deterioration, and extinction. When suffering is destroyed Nirvana is reached, now or after death. Therefore the goal of present life is the removal of suffering through a complex system of moral statutes. In Zen Buddhism, experience is the higher judge than doctrine, the eternal now. It states that perfection (Nirvana) can be achieved at present, whereas another form requires progressive perfection through reincarnation.

2) Salvation is based on one's own actions without any supernatural interventions, i.e. God, though some believe that by works of devotion, the Buddha will give aid.

3) There is no Holy Spirit, only enlightenment of one's self. Truth is subject to one's own "spirit", and all views should be tolerated.

4) There is no sin, only passion (dark) verses enlightenment.

5) Buddha is viewed by various adherents as: Teacher, Great Man, Universal Ruler, and Exalted One. But in all cases, he is simply a part of the eternal and physical universe. There is no creator God (who exists outside of the physical universe).

Christian Teachings and Approaches to Evangelism

1) Buddhism rejects the concept of a creator of the physical universe. This is in direct denial of Romans 1:19, 20 which states that God has revealed himself, his invisible attributes, and his power to all men through the creation.

2) Because they deny the existence of Him as creator, He (God) is not considered their ultimate judge. Without an external judge there can be no absolute right or wrong; sin does not exist. This conflicts with 1 John 1:8, "If we say that we have no sin we are deceiving ourselves."

3) Zen says the ultimate reality of experience and salvation is based on purifying one's own self. Yet, the Bible teaches in Isaiah 1:18 that it is God who judges, forgives, and purifies. Salvation is obtainable only as a free gift of God to those who confess their sins and accept His forgiveness through Jesus Christ.

4) In denying a creator to whom obedience is owed and rejecting sin and its consequence, Buddhism reveals itself to be a self-centered, self-obsessed religion. In witnessing Walter Martin encourages Christians to focus on the depravity of man as revealed in the scriptures, thus confronting the self pride. For example, Romans 3:10-18 quoting Psalm 14 states no man by himself has sought God; all have done evil, all lie and none seek peace. These verses alone give the only adequate explanation for mankind's continual warfare against each other. The discussion could initially center on the attitudes of nations, then races, families, and finally to individuals. Of course this should be done in a respectful, not argumentative manner.

Occult/Cults/Heresies

General Background

The Occult, Cults, and Heresies are a large composite of heterogeneous belief systems that are outside of mainstream Christianity, and are generally not included in the other major religions of the world. Yet, it could be said that anytime a human seeks spiritual experiences apart from God's Spirit they enter into the occult; thus some Hindi, Native American peyote users, and South American Animists (blending Christian concepts with pagan idols) overlap into the occult. Certain aspects of cult worship, e.g. secret Mormon temple rites, and heresies involve the occult ; and all acts of rebellion against God must involve the occult for the scriptures say "rebellion is as the sin of witchcraft"(1 Samuel 15:23). As a general rule, the occult tends to deny the existence of God, cults distort who God the Father or the Trinity is, and heresies confound the deity/humanity of Jesus Christ.

Occult groups, by definition, are secretive; they have hidden rituals, use symbolic language, and communicate with the spiritual realm apart from God. Examples include astrology, psychic readers, Satanists, and the New Age movement.

Cults are defined by Walter Martin as a "group, religious in nature, which surrounds a leader or a group of teachings which either denies or misinterprets essential Bible doctrine." Generally these groups have a dynamic, charismatic leader. He sets up rigid doctrine, usually designed by himself, by which others must adhere. When he uses Biblical terms or concepts, they are taken out of context and are given new meanings. Salvation is usually by works. Revelation from God is felt to be unique, and applicable to each group often through the leader alone. The groups are isolationists, except when evangelizing others. They tend to reject authority outside of the group. Mormonism and the Jehovah Witnesses are well known examples.

Heresies involve aberrant teachings, and their proponents operate within the established Christian Church. It is a complicated subject to decide at times what is heresy and what is simply differing views regarding difficult passages of scripture. Often times a heresy will be known by its fruit over a period of time; does it exalt Christ as Lord? The Arian view of Christ, that He was not divine, would be an example of a heresy. Yet the contested subject of how and when God heals may simply be the result of differing views on the scriptures.

Occult
Background

The occult movement began in the Garden of Eden when Eve (and Adam) listened to Satan. He said they "could be like God" (i.e., as God) and have knowledge apart from Him. Each communed with this rebellious spirit (Satan) and became separated from God's Spirit. This affected their offspring through Cain and others to the present time (Romans 5:12).

The Tower of Babel is the epitome of the occult. Mankind, apart from God, chose as "one" to build their temple of worship - not to God but to symbolize man's prowess (not responsible dominion) over the earth. Countermanding the Word of God to subdue all the earth, they chose to remain in one spot, and rather than to acknowledge God, they made "a name" for themselves. After God dispersed men, they made many towers in various cultures symbolic of the tower of Babel: places of human and animal sacrifices to gods, i.e. demons. The Old Testament and New is replete with examples of the occult, and every person on the face of the earth has experienced it; because of personal rebellion toward God, at one time or another.

The occult is exploding on the face of the earth under a variety of teachers: witch doctors, mediums, gurus, shamans, spiritists, diviners, psychics, palm readers, clairvoyants; and teachings such as astrology, Kabala, Theosophy, types of Hinduism, Masonic Lodge, New Age Movement and some aspects of Native American Religion. Tools that are used include Tarot cards, Ouiji boards, crystals, crystal balls, and tea leaves. Symbols include serpents, scorpions, and a broken, upside-down cross.

Tenets

While the occult is extremely heterogeneous, there are basic teachings to which most adhere.

1) You are god or part of god; the divine is within.
2) Sin is simply not realizing who you are or that you are in disharmony with some other realm of the universe.
3) There is no hell.

4) There are no absolutes; only further enlightenment. Thus all religions are part of a "whole".

5) Life is a continuum, an upward evolutionary progression to spiritual perfection. Reincarnation is simply a process of recycling within this upward movement.

6) Communication with the dead is accepted.

Christian Teaching and Approaches to Evangelism

1) "Rebellion is as the sin of divination (witchcraft)," (1 Samuel 15:23). When man rebels against God's revealed truth, he partakes of occultic powers. God has clearly revealed to all men that he is the Creator, and man has no reasonable right to assume that he (man) is a god or divine. Nature cries out for God and against man. Yet, all lies have a semblance of truth. The Bible says "man has been made in the image of God", but he fell from this by sinning, and then is restored, through faith in Jesus Christ, and thus becomes a "partaker of the divine nature" (2 Peter 1:3,4). God never intended for man to be independent of Him or to supplant Him. This was Satan's idea, and man bas yielded to the temptation throughout the centuries. Christians can boldly say to occultists, "Ye are not gods."

2) Sin is a reality. Hell is a reality (see 2 Peter 2:4-9).

3) Relativism and ecumenism are common in our culture. Josh McDowell bas commented that the "tolerance" of our age is that all views or values be accepted as having an equal weight and consequently all religions should coalesce in unity and harmony, a "rainbow coalition". (He does not support this view.) Religions that have absolutes are excluded, i.e. Christianity and Judaism. Concepts of sin and no sin cannot be in harmony; they are mutually exclusive by a rule of logic. One cannot be a mature Christian and a practicing member of a modem tolerance religious movement.

4) The attraction of the occult is multifold. Its apparent lack of moral absolutes, and its supposed intellectual "open mindedness" appeals to the carnality of man. This is deceiving, since all humans set up absolutes, and all are affected by biased precepts. The real question is whether one submits to God or not. Secondly, and more dangerous, is the desire to experience spiritual things apart from God. Man, born in sin (Psalm 51:5) and unregenerate, communes with Satan (John 8:41-44). It is a true miracle that man, by his volition under God's influence turns from Satan to God. The new birth, the recreation of man's spirit, is a momentous event. Yet the scriptures

say that the "kingdom of God comes without observation," (Luke 17:20).

Satan is a hard taskmaster and he drives people in oppressive fear. But Jesus came and stripped him of his power (Colossians 2:15), so that people might be free from fear (Hebrews 2:14,15), know God as their Father (Romans 8:16), have a confirmation of His love for them by the Holy Spirit (Romans 5:5), and a knowledge that they can live holy lives for him by the strength of Jesus Christ (Philippians 4: 13). The occultist cannot make these promises.

Many thirst for true spirituality (Isaiah 55). If Christians will lead holy, dedicated lives, they, as ambassadors for Christ (2 Corinthians 5:20), can lead many of these people to Him, and He will do true miraculous workings among them.

Cults

Two well known cults are described below; they are a selection out of numerous cults, past and present.

Mormonism

Background Joseph Smith established this group after he claimed to have spoken with God and was given golden tablets in 1820-23, and 1827. This event has been recorded in the Pearl of Great Price. His doctrine was established in the Book of Mormon {published in 1830). It is considered, by followers, as the updated New World equivalent of the Bible. The Doctrine and Covenants was subsequently added. Smith's strange teachings along with his questionable moral character resulted in his fleeing Palmyra, NY, and moving several places until he arrived at Navoo, Illinois. There he was killed by a mob after he and others destroyed a newspaper plant that had exposed his practice of polygamy. Brigham Young led a splintered group from Navoo to Utah. Since then the Mormons have aggressively evangelized people of other faiths.

Tenets (Key concepts in opposition to Christianity)

1) Jesus Christ was not born by miraculous conception, but by physical impregnation of Mary by God.

2) Jesus and Satan were spiritual brothers.

3) Jesus Christ's death and shed blood does not cover all sins (B. Young). There are some sins men must die for themselves, for which Christ's blood cannot forgive

4) By good works within the "church" one can obtain a higher

heavenly position. A type of universal salvation is accepted. When men die, unbelievers go to the lowest heaven, Christians without faith in Joseph Smith to the second heaven and Mormons to the highest heaven. It is largely salvation by works.

5) We can become gods, like and equal to God the Father (polytheism).

6) Polygamy and racism (black skin = more sinful) was promoted in the past.

Christian Teachings and Approaches to Evangelism

The concepts of God and salvation are irreparably damaged if one accepts Smith's teachings. The Bible, in contrast to his teaching, is explicit that Christ was born by miraculous conception (Luke 1:26-35), His shed blood can cover all sins now and eternally (Romans 5:12-21), grace alone saves (Ephesians 2:8) which then leads to good works, and there is only one God (Deuteronomy 6:4, 13-14) not many (though there can be false gods). Paul also refuted polygamy (1 Timothy 3:2), and he denounced racism in that we are all equal in Christ (Galatians 3:26-29).

Thus Joseph Smith was a cultic leader. Why would people follow him? Martin comments that cults draw the lonely and the disenchanted (within the church). Now that there are several generations of Mormons, the offspring know no other faith. Most are well trained in algorithmic rebuttals to any complaints regarding their faith. The Mormon church then as now attracted members by spending considerable effort on family supports. Also, the idea of working one's self to higher positions in heaven has always appealed to the secular mind.

How does one share the true gospel with these people? In truth, some of them find it on their own. The Bible is accepted as a secondary resource in their group. Those reading the true Word of God need encouragement to pursue it. Others mix Joseph Smith and Jesus. Usually, a faithful Christian witness one-on-one may, over time, lead to opportunities to share. Prayer must be included as well.

Jehovah's Witnesses

Background Charles Russell, born in 1852 near Pittsburgh, PA, founded the "Zion's Watch Tower". He separated from the mainstream religious groups over the doctrine of eternal damnation. In 1884 he incorporated his group. He wrote numerous tracts and books. The group named itself (after his death) the Jehovah's Witnesses. Its printing house, the Watch Tower Bible and Tract Society, prints his and others' teachings.

Tenets (Key concepts in opposition to Christianity)
1) They deny the Trinity of God, three parts co-existent, coequal. Jehovah is God alone.
2) The bodily resurrection of Christ is rejected.
3) There is no hell. When a person dies, he is dead, except for a select few.

Christian Teaching and Approaches to Evangelism

1) There has been much criticism against the Watch Tower 's edition of the Bible. For example, the concept of the Trinity is largely deleted, by reconstruction of sentences, e.g. Titus 2:13, 2 Peter 1:1.

2) By denying Christ's physical resurrection from the dead, they undercut the effect of his redemption of man from all aspects of sin: spirit, soul, and body.

3) The denial of the severity of the consequences of sin, e.g. eternal damnation, drastically diminishes the necessity of Christ's death on the cross and the need for Christians to beseech men to be saved. If there is no existence after the grave for the unbeliever, why not eat, drink, and be merry? It also refutes the completeness of Christ's shed blood to cover sin and to redeem us.

As with other cults, hell is denied. Watch Tower adherents are also well-trained in rebuttals. Yet a careful comparison of scriptures between their bible and the Bible can be helpful.

Heresies

Heresies have been combated in the Christian Church since its inception. Most of the conflict has centered around the concept of Jesus Christ as fully God, and as fully man (Colossians 1:18, Hebrews 2:14). In early church history Arius (319 AD) denied the deity of Christ by arguing that he was begotten not eternal. Yet Athanasius rightly argued as the Nicene Creed would say "in One Lord Jesus Christ, the Son of the Father, only begotten, that is, from the substance of the Father, God from God, Light from Light, very God from very God, begotten not made." (John 1:1-4, Colossians 2:9-10). In contrast, the Gnostics would say He was purely divine and not human, yet this conflicted with scriptures such as John 1:14, "the

Word became flesh". The orthodox view of Christ as fully divine and fully human gradually became accepted using Philippians 2:5-11 as the key text.

It was and is vital to correctly understand who Jesus Christ is. For as a man (un-blemished) He could be the sacrifice for the sins of other men, and as God He as part of the triune Godhead could then grant forgiveness for sins.

Other heresies have grown out of sincere Christian attempts to blend Greek philosophy with Christianity. The Greeks believed physical objects represented spiritual realities. In having function follow form, Origen's (250 AD) description of the Trinity placed Jesus Christ at the bottom of a hierarchy, and not as coequal. He also believed that everyone, including the devil, would eventually be saved in contrast to numerous scriptures like 2 Peter 2:4-9, describing hell for the devil, his followers, and those who reject God and Christ.

In recent years a renewed denial of the God/man concept of Jesus Christ is being promoted. According to John Ankerberg, the Jesus Seminar, an ongoing symposia of certain theologians, has stated that Jesus never claimed to be God (contrasted with John 1:1-18, Philippians 2:6), the virgin birth did not occur (refuted by Luke 1: 26-38), Christ did no miracles (in contrast to what the apostle John writes in John 21:24-25), there is not a need for repentance of sins (conflicting with 1 John 1 :8-10), and that he never rose from the dead (refuted by Acts 1:11). Using the claim of scholarship they reject 82% of the sayings attributed to Jesus. They negate that the disciples were eyewitnesses to Christ's teachings, and state that the gospel writings were derived from a "Q" document, a hypothetical pre-gospel text. These approximately 70 theologians have been opposed by numerous others. Many theologians have defended the historical accuracy of the Bible, the textural consistency of the writings, and the conformity of themes between the Old and New Testaments. Also, miracles cannot be refuted simply by denying them (as David Hume attempted to do), and by demanding that Jesus Christ must conform to a naturalistic philosophy (only what we see is real).

J. W. Montgomery says these types of theologians err by 1) consulting only modern authorities without reviewing the historical discussions, 2) neglecting primary documents, 3) begging the question by using a premise that presumes the conclusion, and 4) that they lack knowledge of the context of the times of the writings.

One wonders why these theologians would be interested in the Bible at all. Ankerberg cites certain sources that indicate they have moral and political expedients in doing so. They have attempted to reframe The Christ into a form acceptable to themselves. This reflects the effects of the philosophies of our times: naturalism, relativism, and hedonism (see Chapter 3 Philosophy). The untrained Christian should not be intimidated by their teachings. Jesus said even a child can understand God's principles. Also, there is nothing new under the sun, as Solomon said. The "higher critical views" are simply redressed old heresies. In contrast to the views of "higher criticism", countless scholars, through the centuries, trained in history, linguistics, philosophy, theology, ethics, and science have found the Bible fully reliable and satisfying. And even if they hadn't, "let God be true and every man a liar," (Romans 3:4).

Unitarianism

Background
Unitarians, as a sect distinct from Christian ones, had its origin in the 1500's in Europe. Sect leaders accepted almost any concept of God but rejected the Christian one of the trinity of God. It impacted many Presbyterian Churches in America in the 1700's; and had a tremendous effect among educators in North America in the early to mid 1800's. Horace Mann, a Unitarian, introduced public schools in Massachusetts in 1837. He also developed schools to train teachers. Charles Eliot, as President of Harvard University brought in John Fiske to teach science and history. Both were Unitarian, and because of this propounded an evolution, spiritual and physical, to their students and teachers.

Tenets
1. One God, is revealed through many books and writings: Buddha, Muhammad, Confucius, Lao, Veda are accepted along with the Bible. None of these are infallible.
2. The Concept of trinity denied, Christ is not deity.
3. Salvation is progressive, and works related. "God helps those who help themselves."
4. There is no virgin birth of Christ.
5. No judgment or hell.

6. "God" is evolving the creation to perfection. Fiske promoted this view.

Christian Teachings and Approaches to Evangelism

1) Clearly Unitarianism is contrary to Christian doctrine and is an old heresy traceable to early church times. The Arian heresy denied the full deity of Christ and the Council of Nicaea (325 AD) was convened to refute this. For Jesus said, "He who has seen me has seen the Father," and "I and the Father are One". Paul said Jesus laid aside His glory to come to earth, yet was equal with God. Christ is deity.

2) How can one accept the Bible unless its teachings are accepted? How can it be held that some teachings are divine but others not? Yet the Unitarians do this. Scripture says, "For truly I say to you, until heaven and earth pass away, not the smallest letter or stroke shall pass away from the Law, until all is accomplished" (Matthew 5:18).

3) The Bible also teaches clearly about hell, where there will be "gnashing of teeth". "For unless you believe that I am He, you shall die in your sins" (John 8:24). Proverbs 14:12 says, "There is a way which seems right to a man but its end is the way of death."

4) The virgin birth of Christ is troubling to many non-Christian faiths, but is an essential doctrine. Jesus had to have a blemish free body, to be the once for all sacrifice. His miraculous conception accomplished this. Being born as a sinless man from woman He could then crush the head of Satan (Genesis 3:14-16; Colossians 2:13-15), stripping him of his power in the earth. The virgin birth is important.

5) The Unitarian doctrines appeal to the carnal educated mind. It allows one "to do his own thing", "think his own way", and still supposedly be accepted by God. It espouses reason, logic even in conflict with Biblical commands.

Because these adherents walk in the self pride of their own intellect and believe in self-salvation, they can be very difficult to reach with the message of God's holiness, judgment and mercy. They may lead exemplary lives and be pillars in the community, but they walk in darkness if they do not accept the cleansing of God's Spirit. They need to see examples of true Christian love, humility, integrity and a willingness to serve God no matter the cost; there is a need in every human heart for the Spirit of God.

Native American Religions – Traditional
Example: The Navajo

Background

According to traditional Navajo lore, The People (Dine') have always lived in the area between four sacred mountains of the Four Corners area of Utah, New Mexico, Arizona, and Colorado. Their history and religion are essentially one (see below). According to current sociologic and anthropologic views, they probably are part of a people group who migrated from Alaska and Canada about 1000 AD. This would be consistent with the view that after the flood groups of people migrated into all parts of the world, including some that migrated across India to China then across the Bering Strait to Alaska, Canada, and finally the southwest United States. Initially an agrarian society, they have become increasingly involved in cottage industries such as jewelry and rug making. Mining of coal and uranium has been important too.

Tenets

1) Religion, social, and economic issues are all part of a unified system; that is, one affects the other. Example: harmony with nature (and Holy People) brings health.

2) Beings are divided into Earth Surface People (who we are) and Holy People (supernatural; powerful, mysterious, like gods, yet not all knowing or all powerful, and can be capricious). There are accounts of a creator god, be'gochidi', but the primary important "beings" are the Holy People especially Changing Woman. She is favorable to, and has taught Surface People how to control wind, lightning, storms, and animals through various ceremonies (including the Blessing Way).

3) There is a story of a flooding of the earth after the quarreling of the Holy People when they lived below the earth's surface. This caused them to come to the surface. Death, and the Surface People occurred at this time; first man, first woman were created from ears of corn by the Holy People.

4) Surface People must always have intermediaries between them and the Holy People. It is necessary to regularly appease certain Holy People, e.g., disease may represent a violation of a taboo, or an attack by the Holy People, a ghost, or a witch. Divination is required to discern which it is. Certain Surface People (approximately 1 in 6) are

given a "gift" to divine using star gazing (reading messages in crystals), hand trembling, or through use of narcotic plant matter (peyote). A ceremony, including the use of songs and prayers within a defined ritualism (often complex), is performed and the curse discerned. A "sing", with a "singer", is prescribed for healing or resolution of the problem.

There are a multitude of taboos, ba'hadzid, some which are based on practical experience, others based on fears of the unknown. Witches and ghosts are often involved. Ghosts are dead Surface People, lurking in a shadowy uninviting afterworld. The malignant part of a person comes out in a ghost and Surface People must "avoid" certain taboos to appease them, e.g. avoiding looking at the grave of someone; and if the ghost is angered, a ceremony must be done to be set free. Witches, certain Surface People, cast spells to cause illness or rob the property of other Surface People. To be protected from these spells, ceremonies like the Enemy Way "squaw dance" is performed.

5) Ceremonies or Chants are very important to the traditionalist. They may be performed hundreds of times in their life time. A chant can last days, involve many family and extended family, vary in cost from hundreds to thousands of dollars.

Christian Teachings and Approaches to Evangelism

1) Because of the recent history of the Anglo-American dominance in North America, evangelism should be conducted from a heart of true concern, individual to individual. Many Native Americans tend to view Christianity in the light of past wrongs and as a white man's religion. Craig Smith (a Native American) says it is important to associate it, evangelism, with the Jewish history of a nomadic tribe, a minority often under subjection to the dominant society (Rome), and much persecuted. As such it is not a white man's religion and Native Americans may be better able to identify with it. Accordingly, he feels North American Natives can more easily relate with and evangelize those Indian groups in South America.

2) As with all historical religions, i.e. present before the Jewish law or the Christian gospel were presented to the people group, beliefs are the result of oral (or written) teachings passed from generation to generation. The teachings contain, in varying degrees of purity, the concepts given from the creation of Adam and Eve to the time of the Noah dispersion. All cultures have retained concepts

of a creator, blood sacrifice, redeemer, flood after evil done, etc. These can be emphasized and used as a starting point of discussion in revealing to a person that the Bible is the further, final, and purist form of God's revelation to man.

3) In the traditional way death is viewed as horrible. People are to avoid looking at anything dead; there is a great fear of death. This is certainly true among all cultures, but the Bible says in Hebrews 2:14-15, "Since then the children share in flesh and blood, He himself likewise also partook of the same, that through death He might render powerless him who had the power of death, that is, the devil; and might deliver those who through fear of death were subject to slavery all their lives." How does He do this? He calls all who confess Him as Lord, and accept His forgiveness of sin (Romans 10:10), as His children. He then promises to never leave nor forsake them, and that He has prepared a wonderful heaven for them, not a shadowy uninviting place (as viewed by some traditionalists).

4) Most traditional Native American faiths have polytheistic views, whether they are called gods or not. Crying Wind (from the Kickapoo tribe) lists the wind god, bear god, snake and homed toad god, etc. These gods can be kind or malevolent, and certainly not directly approachable. Yet the Bible reveals a God who is pure, holy, and His thoughts are towards man for good. He never changes, and does not need appeasement. As the Creator, He allows man to directly approach Him through Jesus Christ; but only by confession and repentance. Once forgiven through the trusting of Christ as savior, there is neither Anglo nor Native American Indian; all are equal before God.

5) There can be great fear regarding witches and ghosts among traditionalists. Yet Jesus said to His followers, "Behold I have given you authority to tread upon serpents and scorpions and over all the power of the enemy, and nothing shall injure you," (Luke 10:19). The Native American (and anyone else) who trusts Christ can reject demonic influence in their own lives and their families' lives.

In summary, the Bible if presented in humility, individually, and with a certain cultural sensitivity can bring great joy to those Native Americans who desire to know God better. They in turn can take it to other people groups as co-laborers in Christ.

Eastern Religions – Hindu

Background

There was no one founder of Hinduism. It developed in India. There are hundreds to thousands of sects, all considered part of the One Eternal System (sanatana dharma). The earliest collection of Hindu scripture, The Vedas (meaning wisdom or knowledge) were compiled around 1000 BC. There are two basic groups, the ritualistic and the philosophic. Ritualistic followers worship and sacrifice to Vedic gods in elaborate and precisely followed ceremonies, so as to gain the most benefits. The Brahmas are part of this group. Philosophic followers adhere to the mystical meaning of the rites rather than form.

These Hindu writings have been added to and recompiled. In 700 BC the Vedanta or interpretations of the Vedas were developed. The Bhagavad-Gita was added in 200 BC, and in 800 AD the writings were combined. L. Renou feels that Hindi writings have impacted Buddhism, Islam, and other Southeastern Asian religious sects.

Hare-Krishna is an offshoot of the Vishna, and Transcendental Meditation is a monistic, atheistic form of Hinduism. Both utilize repetitive prayers called "mantras". Spiritual leaders are called gurus.

Tenets

1) There are many gods or a single God. God, or gods, are in all, and are all. This is both pantheism and monotheism. There are also forms of atheism as well which states that the universe is one physical substance without a spiritual dimension (in this Buddhism can overlap Hinduism).

One writing popular today, the Bhagavad-Gita states there are numerous gods with one central God. Among these are the warrior gods, avatars, who help those who live in the maya ("illusion" – physical world). Krishna is the leading avatar; yet he is not completely pure, moral, or holy.

In the combined Vedantic writings, Brahman is the Supreme One, who is all in all, devoid of all attributes, yet within him exist being, consciousness, and bliss. This concept has been further delineated into the god Vishna. Followers of Vishnu believe Krishna is an incarnation of this god.

2) The concluding chapters of the Vedas (lpanishads) state that by works all mankind can achieve the divine state. In this form of

Hinduism the spiritual is more real than the physical, and one's individual condition must be denied or "shed" (the maya or illusion) so that the real self may become one in the "sea of the One Reality, God". This shedding of self involves karma, "an inexorable law of retributive justice", a law of cause and effect. As one purifies himself, goodness and elevation toward the divine state is achieved. Numerous cycles of reincarnation (called samsara) may be required to reach perfection.

3) Salvation, or reaching perfection and pure karma can currently be obtained by three pathways.

    a. Karma marga emphasizes ritualistic purification of self.

    b. Bhakti marga requires purification by devotion to a particular god or gods.

    c. Juara marga develops an inward self-realization to break free from the illusion (maya–physical) and perceive one's true self without a god's help.

4) Moral behavior may be ascetic or licentious, depending on one's beliefs.

Christian Teachings and Approaches to Evangelism

1) The teachings of Hinduism are very convoluted and allow almost any concept of god or non-god; thus it cannot include Christianity which says that Jehovah is the one true God. The Bible describes God as pure, holy, just, merciful, never able to sin or even appear sinful; this does not fit the description of the avatars of Hinduism. Yoga is spiritually dangerous to Christians.

2) Salvation in the Bible is a gift of God, not a purifying by self works. Good works are the result or manifestation of salvation to the Christian, but the Hindi must always be attempting and never quite attaining, self purification. Their sin is always before them.

3) For the Christian, heaven involves real individuals with intimate relationships to a personal God, not an amorphous bliss as in Hinduism.

4) As with all other religious groups, Hinduism reflects knowledge of early Biblical concepts (the flood, creation, etc.). But these are grotesque and distorted in contrast to the majestic descriptions of Genesis. In the Satapatha-Brahmana, one story about the flood describes how a fish spoke to a teacher. If he protected the fish, it would protect him from the great flood by telling him when to build a boat and that he would guide him to a mountain where the

boat could rest as the flood subsided. While some resemblance remains, it lacks the majesty and authenticity of the story of God judging the sins of man, of saving the one who would listen to Him, and how He preserved the animal kingdom through him (Noah). Another, a creation story describes the waters of the earth that became troubled within themselves, and produced a golden egg. First man was also produced. He broke the egg open and floated in it. As he began to speak he created gods and demons, day and night, and self reproductive power. In this we can see the distorted remnants of the Spirit of God forming day/night, the stars, then the animals, and giving man the responsibility of naming and ruling over them.

There are numerous other Hindi renderings of the flood, creation, and blood sacrifices. These are strong anthropologic evidence for a common origin of man. But the Hindi legends are, as in other cultures, distorted from the pure and holy ones described in the Bible. In particular, the understanding of God's nature, His interaction with man, and the concept and results of sin are confused. Yet the Christian can use the historical stories of Genesis in evangelism.

Without an accurate knowledge of God, there cannot be an intimate relationship with Him, and without this relationship there cannot be peace. As with any of the mystical or experience based religions, sharing one's own subjective experiences with God may not be useful, as it may become "who's got the best experience". One needs to approach the Hindi with compassion, a consistent lifestyle of devotion to God. Then opportunities may arise to share timely and accurate scriptural principles. As William Carey (missionary, early 1800's, India) said, "So far as our experience goes in this work, we must freely acknowledge that every Hindu among us who has been gained to Christ has been won by the astonishing and all-constraining love exhibited in our Redeemer's propitiatory death." If Christ be lifted up, He will draw all men to himself.

Islam

Background

Muhammad was born in 570 AD within an influential family in Mecca, Arabia. Both parents died when he was young. He was raised by an uncle. It is stated that he lived morally clean as a young man and married (Khadija). After she died he then began the practice of polygamy. In his search to understand religious issues, he met both Christians and Jews and respected the Bible (Christians are called People of the Book by many Muslims). Yet at one point during the month of Ramadan (time of occurrence varies), while meditating and praying, he stated that he received revelation and instructions from the archangel Gabriel. These formed the basis of the Qur'an. Further writings were included in the "Hadiths". He stated that these writings were the final superior revelation, which superseded and corrected previous writings, including the Bible, from the one Supreme God. He died in 632 AD.

Tenets

1) Each Muslim must follow the "5 Pillars": reciting the creed (shahada), prayer (salat), alms giving (sahat), fasting (saum), and pilgrimage (hajj) to Mecca.

2) Salvation is based on self-righteousness, that is, on the Day of Judgment do the good deeds outweigh the bad ones? However, if ones dies as a martyr in a Jihad (Holy War) salvation is assured. The death of Christ on a cross for sins is rejected, as well as his resurrection and deity. He is important as a prophet, but only one of 124,000. Muhammad is the supreme prophet, "The Praised One".

3) There is one God, supreme, creator of all things, Allah.

4) Ramadan. A holy time, in remembrance of the time of revelations given to Muhammad. The time varies; the Muslim calendar varies year to year. It is a time of "striving or doing battle against your inner desires ..." It is a private arrangement between you and God." Each adherent is to fast from sunrise to sunset with abstention from food, drink, smoking, marital sex. Prayers occur each night culminating in the haylat al-Qadi, "Night of Power or Destiny." The Eid-al-Fitr is a 3-day feast at the end.

Christian Teachings and Approaches to Evangelism

1) Muhammad wrote his revelations after being exposed to the

Bible. It is not surprising therefore, that while many Muslims accept the Bible as a sacred writing, it is given lower prestige than his own writings. How can Jesus Christ's writings be of less importance than Muhammad's, when Jesus said, "He who has seen me has seen the Father," and "I am the way, and the truth, and the life; no one comes to the Father but through me" (John 14:9; 14:6)? Muhammad's writings cannot be of a greater importance, if one accepts the teachings of Jesus. Jesus is not one of many lesser prophets, and it may be useful to mention this if a Muslim respects the Judea-Christian scriptures.

2) For Muhammad (and his followers) God is distant and impersonal. Once, during a discussion between Muslim and Christian friends, the Muslim asked, "Have you ever wondered what God looks like, for we are not allowed to look on Him? There is a great veil that separates Him from us." The Christian was able to say, "Yes, Jesus is God's Son, and He reveals the Father to us." To the Christian, God is not distant, or impersonal. Jesus has bridged the gulf between God and man as intercessor, and has given God's Holy Spirit as a comforter and guide to the Christian.

The Muslim has difficulty thinking of God as Father, he is aware of his sins, and yet has no firm assurance of forgiveness and salvation. Romans 8:14,15 says that as believers in Christ we have God's Spirit bearing witness that He is our Father and we are his children by adoption. Our sins are fully forgiven as we confess them and we have assurance of salvation (Romans 10:9-11 and 1 John 1:9). We can offer the Muslim these great promises which are available to all men for the scripture says "Whoever believes in Him will not be disappointed" (Romans 10:11).

3) As is true in evangelism within any culture, respect for the people, having concern for them personally is very important. Many Muslims have a respect for the Bible, thus Christians should respectfully and truthfully use it, when discussing sacred issues.

Judaism

Background

The Jewish people are an historical people whose origin dates to the time of Abraham, approximately 2000 BC. Towns like Ur, Haran, and Nahor which are associated with the patriarchs are well documented in the secular literature. The Bible records that Abraham was called by the one true God to move from Ur to what is now present-day Israel. There his offspring arose as a nation. As a nation it was supposed to be separated unto this God in contrast to the other polytheistic ones in that time and era. The Old Testament is an account of the repeated failures of the people to do so, and God's warning, punishment, and then healing of them. There have been three dispersions of the people due to their rebellion. The last occurred just after the death of Christ. The re-collecting of the Jewish people back to Israel has been occurring since the early 1900's, and especially after World War II when Israel became a nation in 1948, in fulfillment of prophesies.

The rebuilding of the Jewish state has been greatly contested and the scene of recurrent wars with the Muslim dominated Arab states around it. This too is in fulfillment of prophesy that Israel would become a "heavy stone" to the nations (Zechariah 12:3), and the spiritual offshoot of the conflict between Jacob and Esau until the end of time. The nation of Israel now has a population of 13 million people in 8,000 square miles of land (approximately 250 miles by 40 miles).

The teachings of Judaism, particularly the Pentateuch (Torah), form the foundations of the Christian faith, and some of the foundations of Islam. The Jews themselves hold other documents, as well, to be necessary to religious life. These are the Mishnah and Gemara which make up the Talmud, the legal, ritualistic, and ethical teachings (written between 200 BC and 500 AD). There are three main religious subgroups: 1) Orthodox accept the Torah and Talmud, 2) Reform accept the Torah but consider the Talmud of human origin, and 3) Conservative accept Torah, Talmud, but that they must be relevant to current times. Judaism comprises a religion, race, and social group.

Tenets

1) M. Steinberg comments that Judaism has no specific creeds because it is a culture which encourages freedom of thought, and pursues the "good life" – justice and mercy. Thus to many, Judaism pursues ethics (relationships among man) first, and doctrine (concepts of God) second.

2) The one doctrinal statement that is accepted by many Jews is the reality of the one true God. Yet, He can be personal, abstract (according to Maimonides, an early Jewish teacher) or to some there is no God. At best, he can only be partly understood.

3) Among God-fearing Jews, He is Creator, Lawgiver, Guide to history, Helper, Liberator, Savior.

4) Salvation is primarily referred to as deliverance from evil in this present world. It can be "man's victory over his limitations". God guides and assists him in this. Many still hope for the return of the Messiah, to fully deliver them. Heaven is generally ill-defined.

5) Strong emphasis is placed on moral conduct in the Torah/Talmud. Examples include: Hillel (about 10 AD) stated that "which is hurtful to thee do not to thy neighbor". And Akiba (about 200 AD), said the great principle of Judaism is, "Thou shalt love thy neighbor as thyself" (Leviticus).

6) Rituals are important to many. Rituals reflect a life committed to God.

Christian Teachings and Approaches to Evangelism

1) Obviously, with the Old Testament being the foundation of both Christianity and Judaism, there is considerable overlap of beliefs among those who accept the Scriptures as divine revelation from God. However the Jewish people are very heterogeneous:

   a. Some do not accept the scriptures as divine at all. These are secular Jews born into Judaism. They must be approached as one approaches a humanist (see previous discussion).

   b. Others have great anger and/or sorrow towards God due to the severe persecution that the Jewish people have undergone.

It is felt by most Christian scholars that the Jewish people were chosen by God, not for their good works, but because he desired a people to which he could reveal his faithfulness and nature. These people were to respond to Him with love and appreciation and He would bless them (book of Deuteronomy). The non-Jewish people of the world would see this, and desire God as well. Unfortunately, the Old Testament is a saga of the Chosen People rebelling against God. Because of God's holiness He punished them, but by His mercy restored them. After their (and the Gentile's) rejection of Him (Jesus) the Jews were dispersed into all the earth until He should call them back at the end of the age.

The scriptures say that one day the people of the Jewish nation will realize that Jesus is the Messiah and convert to Him in mass (Zechariah 12:10). Until then, as a nation, a veil (concerning Jesus' messiahship) remains over their eyes (1 Corinthians 3:15). This is of course a point of great contention for them. Jews for Jesus and other organizations are very much at the front of an evangelistic effort to help fellow individual Jews believe. It is difficult to say, "your people have suffered because of their rebellion". Nonetheless, it is true. As well, what does one say to, "My parents died in the Holocaust. Where are they now?" Paul the Apostle was greatly distressed over this same issue stating that he would allow himself to be cut off from God if only his people would believe (Romans 9). It must be remembered that God is just, holy, and merciful and He deals with each man based on how that person has responded to the light given him (see the book of Romans 1 and 2). Christians can beseech the Jewish people to consider the claims of Jesus as the Messiah. If they're willing to listen, there is an impressive list of Old Testament prophecies fulfilled in the life of Christ (see **Figure 3**). If not, Christians must lead holy lives before them.

It should be remembered that Christians, or some of those who have professed to be, have at times in history, persecuted the Jews. As well, in early church history the Jews persecuted Christians. How could this be? God has said, "I will bless those who bless you, and the one who curses you I will curse." (Genesis 12:3) Also, the Jews, as Paul said are our spiritual forebears and the early church was then composed of Jewish leaders. Therefore, we must always support the Jewish people in prayer and in deed. Better understanding of Jewish customs will assist Christians in more effective evangelism.

2) Jesus is the fulfillment of hundreds of Old Testament prophecies. Derek Prince compares Moses' life with Jesus'; for in Deuteronomy 18:18-19 God says, "I will raise up a prophet from among the brethren like unto thee; (Moses) and I will put My words in his mouth, and he shall speak unto them all that I shall command

him. And it shall come to pass, that whosoever will not hearken unto My words which he shall speak in my name, I will require it of him." Paul in Acts 3:22-26 applies these words to Jesus. Prince compares them according to childhood, character, personal experience and ministry. Examples of each are given in **Figure 3**.

FIGURE 3

Moses	Childhood	Jesus
Ex. 1:15-16	cruel king tried to kill	Matt. 2:16
Ex. 2:2	faith of parents saved child	Matt. 7:13-14
Acts 7:42	as child had wisdom/understanding	Luke 2:46-47

	Character	
Num. 12:3	meek	Matt. 11:29

	Personal Experience	
Ex. 2:14	rejected by Israel for a time	Matt. 27:21-22
Ex. 2:15, 21	received by Gentiles when rejected by Israel	Acts 13:44-48
Num. 12:7-8	spoke face to face with God	John 1:18
Jude 9	burial place guarded by angel	Matt. 28:2-6
Matt. 17:3	appeared to those after death	John 20:19-20

	Ministry	
Deut. 4:1	teacher/prophet	Matt. 5:1-2
Ex. 3:7-10	brought deliverance	Luke 4:17-21
Ex. 15:25-26	brought healing	Matt. 4:23
Ex. 24:7-8	established covenant between God and His people	Matt. 26:26-28

Other relevant scriptures regarding Jesus as the Messiah :

Old Testament	Identification of Christ	New Testament
Micah 5:2	born in Bethlehem	Matt. 2:1-8
Isa. 7:14	born of a virgin	Matt. 1:20-23
Isa. 42:1-4	faithful servant	Matt. 12:14-21
Isa. 6:9-10	Christ not recognized by Jewish people	Matt. 13:13-15 Matt. 13:54-58
Zech. 9:9	King of Jews will enter Jerusalem on foal of a donkey	Matt. 21:1-11
Zech. 11:12-13	betrayed for thirty pieces of silver	Matt. 16:14-16 Matt. 27:3-10
Isa. 53	crucifixion of Christ	Matt. 26 & 27 Mark 15 Luke 22 & 23
Psalm 22	sufferings of Christ	Matt. 27 John 19
Psalm 16:10	resurrection of body of Christ	Luke 24 John 20, 21 Mark 16 Matt. 28

Many Jews search the scriptures, longing for Messiah. As seen in the above scriptures, Jesus Christ of Nazareth fulfilled the requirements. We, as Christians, can expound on the above scriptures to exhort them to believe in Him.

Christianity

Background

The world began around 4004 BC according to Bishop Ussher using Biblical chronology as a guide. There is nothing scientific or scriptural to argue against this date, even though it professes to be only a close approximation.

Moses wrote what is called the Pentateuch (Genesis, Exodus, Leviticus, Numbers, and Deuteronomy) somewhere around 1400 BC. Using evidence such as the phrase "and these are the generations" as an indication of a series of written histories, many scholars believe Moses compiled the writings and oral records then available to him.

Subsequent authors "wrote under the inspiration of the Holy Spirit", throughout the next 1500 years. The Bible has a book of beginning (Genesis) and ending (Revelation).

The Bible contains the best historical writings known with hundreds of archeological findings confirming comments in it. Often skeptics have derided its accuracy until an archeological object has been found that supported it. Also, there are extant manuscripts (Dead Sea Scrolls, and early church letters) that confirm its accurate transmission down through two millennia. See **Figure** 4, "Bible Documents Timeline."

The Bible is divided into "Old" and "New" Testaments. Christianity and Judaism part on these. Judaism accepts only books written and compiled before Christ, the Old Testament, and Christians are those who accept both the Old and New Testaments (the New Testament describes the activities of Jesus' life and its impact among His followers). There are numerous sects of Christianity with differing views on such issues as healing, speaking in tongues, the process of sanctification, etc. However, all true sects of Christianity will adhere to certain fundamental tenets and these have been clarified and consolidated into such writings as the Apostle's Creed (200-300 AD), Nicene Creed (325 AD), etc. The Creeds grew out of the necessity to combat heresies (see Occult/ Cults/ Heresies) and to generally unify the Church.

Tenets

1) There is one God.

2) He is supreme over heaven, earth, and the universe as the creator.

3) He is composed of a trinity: Father, Son (Jesus Christ), and the Holy Spirit.

4) Jesus Christ: God's Son, born of a virgin, died for the sins of man, descended into hell, was raised on the third day, he ascended into heaven, and is seated at God's right hand. God will judge mankind through Jesus Christ.

5) The Holy Spirit is given to those who accept Jesus Christ as Savior and Lord. He is the spirit of truth, and guides the believer and comforts him. The secular man is convicted by the Holy Spirit of sin, righteousness and judgment to come.

6) God the Father is Ruler of all.

7) Man, God's creation in His image, rebelled (sinned) against Him. Adam, the first man yielded to the influence of Satan, a fallen angel. By doing so he became in union with Satan and separated from God. This nature passed to his offspring.

8) The sins of an individual can be forgiven by accepting the suffering of Christ in the person's place (called substitutionary atonement).

9) If a person's sins are forgiven, he or she is transferred from Satan's union to direct relationship with God the Father through Jesus Christ by the power of the Holy Spirit, and is considered His child. The person's spirit is "re-generated" to be "born again."

10) God's children will live with Him, after death, forever. Those who have not become His children are sent to everlasting hell (separation from God).

Christian Teachings and Apologetics

1) The Bible presents a majestic, time specific and historically reliable history of the beginnings and purpose of the physical universe. Genesis is not a myth. In contrast, myths such as the Epic of Gilgamesh (Syrian) have an ambiguous onset of the beginning of the universe. Its concept of the character(s) of god or gods is blended with that of fallen human attributes and even bizarre monstrous ones, whereas in the Bible God is pure, holy, and above reproach. The Hindi have gods that are devious and cannot be fully trusted. This causes them to have a fear and distrust for the one true God. However, Christians can trust that He is not subject to human foibles; what He says He means, and means what He says.

2) As Creator, God is able and has set the rules and principles by

which His creation operates. This brings a constancy and purpose to life. The atheist in contrast by denying a creator, thus attempts to set his own rules, which are relative, constantly shifting and create chaos resulting in no lasting purpose to life. The Christian can present to every man a God who is reliable, loving, able to intervene to help all who call upon Him; yet who is also just and holy and will judge those who rebel against Him.

3) Many ask, how can Christians expect the Bible to apply to all societies, and peoples? A partial answer is that God in times past revealed Himself to mankind through creation, but has now revealed Himself more perfectly and specifically in the man Jesus Christ. Evangelism of those of other faiths must be based on our desire for them to know God personally: by experiencing the rebirth of their spirit, having the burden of sin removed, and by receiving a hope of eternal life after death. God is no respecter of persons; all have sinned, and yet all have the opportunity to receive His great and precious promises.

4) Christianity answers the issues of life better than any other belief system. It gives standards of conduct such as don't lie, steal, etc. (as do many other faiths), but it goes beyond to say that God's Spirit will guide those who trust Him into all truth. The Christian thus has God's written word, and His spoken word (the Spirit of God in his heart) to guide him in the affairs of life. As well the Spirit of God gives the Christian strength to do this. This brings great constancy and peace. Christians should desire others to experience this, and should encourage one another.

5) The Bible accurately deals with the spirit realm. There is a devil. It is difficult to fully understand many of the actions of mankind without acknowledging the influence of the spiritual realm. Leaders of nations throughout the ages have promised each other peace only to immediately "stab one another in the back." Why? The Bible states that until a man is "born again" by God's Spirit, he is under the influence, and in fact, in communion with Satan's spirit (John 8:44, 1 John 3:8-10). Thus, he (man) is a slave to Satan and sin. It says in Luke 4:18 that Christ came to set the captives free, and that Christians now, as ambassadors for Him, have that same responsibility (Mark 16:15-18). Elsewhere it is said, "Behold, I have given you authority to tread on serpents and scorpions and over all the power of the enemy. Go therefore and make disciples of all the

nations." "Whatsoever you shall bind on earth shall be bound in heaven; and whatever you loose on earth shall be loosed in heaven" (Luke 10:19, Matthew 28:18-20, Matthew 18:18). Christians no longer need to fear Satan or death, and others need this good news.

Conclusion

Don Richardson, long time missionary and writer (Eternity in Their Hearts) says 95% of cultures have a concept of a creator (Theos). As it says in Romans 1, God has revealed Himself to all men through the creation. Thus the first step in evangelism of any person is: does this person believe in a creator? If yes, a bridge across cultures can be crossed by discussing concepts such as the world wide flood and the need for blood sacrifices. From this one can proceed as the Apostles did with the Jews, preaching Christ crucified for sins. If the answer is no, then one must review the evidences for a creation, and thus a creator (see "Why I Believe in God and Not Evolution").

Richardson also points out that not all of a pagan culture is necessarily "worthless". For example, late 19th century evangelism of Native Americans involved removing some of the children from their homes, prohibiting them from speaking their language and requiring them to wear European style clothing. Preaching and teaching the gospel does not require this, and in fact has created a situation today where many Native Americans view Christianity as simply a "White Man's Religion" rather than as God's message to mankind. It is important to understand another's culture, and to respect and leave alone those things not directly addressed in God 's Word; often natives of the culture who have converted to Christianity are best able to discern this.

In conclusion, Christianity is the final, specific, and purist revelation of God to man. It answers the great religious questions of how and why the universe was made, man's true origins and purpose on earth, and where one goes after death. We have, as believers in Christ, great reasons for hope, and thus we can labor in love by acts of faith among those in our community that they too might come to know the true, personal, Almighty God.

FIGURE 4 – Bible Documents Timeline

BC   > 100 BC Numerous Biblical references on tablets, disks, building blocks.

100 BC Fragments from Dead Sea Scrolls (portions of all OT books except Esther) leather, copper.

AD   35-700 AD Fragments (25 of 27 OT books, 40% of NT text) both papyri and parchment, written in Latin, Syriac, Egyptian Earliest NT fragment - 125 AD from the book of John. Masoretic (Hebrew) text 600-950 AD OT.

200-300 AD Septuagint Greek OT.

340-420 AD Vulgate Latin OT/NT (Jerome).

1380 Wycliffe's translation of Bible into English. Sent out Lollard preachers - many burned at stake.

1450 Guttenberg Press published Latin Vulgate. All Bibles handwritten until this time.

1467 Erasmus translates NT from Latin to Greek and places in double columns. Allows for reading of scripture among Greek trained theology students - especially at Cambridge.

1526 William Tyndale translates NT into common English. He said, "If God spare my life, ere many years, I will cause a boy that driveth the plow to know more of the scriptures than thou dost." (in reference to the clergy). He was chased about Europe. He was finally caught, strangled, and burned at the stake. His last statement, "Lord, open the eyes of the king."

1536 Martin Luther's German translation for the common man.

1537 Matthew's Bible translated by John Rogers using essentially Tyndale's NT text. It was approved by King Henry VIII. (The king's eyes were opened.) It contained commentary notes as well.

1539 Coverdale Bible translated by Miles Coverdale, softened some of Roger's commentary. Approved by the king. A large copy was chained to a pedestal in every church; also called the Great Bible.

1560 Geneva Bible also called the Breeches Bible. Used by the Pilgrims.

1611 King James Bible team headed up by Richard Bancroft utilized 50-60 translators. King James I was king.

More recent translations:
        English Revised Version   1881
        American Standard Version   1901
        New American Standard Version   1971
        New International Version   1978

Note: OT= Old Testament of the Bible
        NT= New Testament of the Bible

42

FIGURE 5 – Bible Pages From Different Dates

100 BC   Book of Noah on Papyrus

300-500 AD   Uncial Script on Papyrus

1200 AD   Genesis 8 on Vellum

1615 AD   Breeches Bible

CHAPTER 3

PHILOSOPHY

Introduction

The term philosophy comes from two Greek words: philos - friend, and sophos - wise. Thus it embraces the idea of one who loves or desires knowledge, understanding, and wisdom. This usually comprises both value-commitments and beliefs about the general nature of things. The process by which one philosophizes is called reasoning.

Reasoning is a mental process by which a person assesses both himself, others and his environment. It is both inductive and deductive (see definitions in science section). By it he compares and contrasts, associates and disassociates information. Evidencing is a type of reasoning. One sees a car, therefore it is. Motivation affects reason. For example, one dislikes walking long distance, and a car becomes viewed as a necessity of life. Causality is a process of reasoning. A car runs on gas therefore it must have gas to run. Philosophy as a construct can be isolated to assessing only the physical realm (excluding the spiritual) as occurs currently in naturalism, previously in positivism (1800's). It can emphasize mental perception as promoted by David Hume in the 1700's. It can exclude or minimize the physical, emphasizing the spiritual as forms of New Ageism. Other world views, including Christianity, accept the physical, mental and spiritual realm as areas to be examined.

Reasoning requires 4 main assumptions:
1) that truth can be discovered
2) that reality is real (physical and/or spiritual), and can be understood
3) man is finite in his capacity for understanding knowledge
4) corollary: revelation from God is necessary for understanding absolute truth.

As will be shown, secular philosophy fails to address at least one or more of the first three assumptions, but Christianity is fully satisfying of all four. Some common examples of secular and Christian philosophy are reviewed.

Definitions

Most relevant terms are defined in the text. But some other useful terms are listed below:

Allegory: an illumination of ideas as people, animals, or places. Example: In Pilgrim's Progress different tests/temptations are represented as beings.

Analogy: an extended comparison of the similarities between two seemingly dissimilar things. Example: The use of a car and driver to describe the body and spirit of a person.

Dichotomy: a separation of ideas, things into two separate groupings, e.g. God and man; man and nature.

Fact: an observation generally available to all to confirm. It does not always imply reproducibility. Example: True miracles are facts; for example in the Bible the lame man known to all before he was healed, and who then walks, demonstrates a fact.

Knowledge: the acquisition of facts.

Solipsism: propounded by Hume and others that the only thing that self can know is self. Example: "Know thyself', or "Truth is in the eyes of the beholder". It is a self-centered construct.

Sophistry: having the appearance of truth when it is not. Example: To present a weak or false concept in complicated terms. Many of the arguments used to justify evolution are sophistry. To illustrate, there has never been an observed transition from reptile to bird; yet books are written just on that topic.

Syncretism: the blending of conflicting philosophies or ideas into a "unified" whole. Example: The New Age movement (see Religion).

Understanding: the process of categorization and context of knowledge.

Wisdom: the application of facts, knowledge, and understanding to a given situation.

General Overview

Francis Schaeffer outlines the progression of secular and religious philosophy and their impact on society in a wonderfully concise way in two books, *Escape from Reason* and *How Should We Then Live*.

He states that the <u>classical philosophers</u> (Socrates, Plato, Aristotle) followed 3 principles. The first was called rationalism, the idea that man can gather information concerning particulars and then formulate universal concepts (a form of induction). The second principle was, all is rational, e.g. A is not non-A; that is, a thing cannot "be" and "not be" at the same time (later philosophers would reject this). And third, they had a hope that all knowledge could be unified. He points out that because they did not, by and large, accept Biblical views of God, they failed to unite tangible and intangible concepts. As a subgroup the Atomists believed that only matter exists and that there is no God or spirit realm. Democritus and Empedodes were leaders. These views have affected man's thinking even until this day.

After the time of the classical philosophers until Thomas Aquinas (1225-1274), <u>Byzantine</u> philosophy reigned. It emphasized the heavenly as perfect and spurned the earthly as corrupt. Schaeffer reviews art of this period noting that heaven was considered so holy that it was pictured symbolically, and earthly images were largely ignored. Dante's writings reflect this dichotomy; he struggled through Purgatory assisted by Virgil, representing secular reason. Beatrice (a saint) then assisted him into heaven. Later Aquinas, influenced by Aristotle, acknowledged that the earth was God's creation as well. He developed the dichotomy: Grace/Nature. Grace involved man's soul (mind and intellect), spirit, and God; whereas nature comprised the physical creation. He felt that while man's body and will were fallen, his intellect was not. At this time art began to become more realistic, e.g. Giotto, Van Eyck.

The <u>Renaissance</u> branched out from Aquinas's time by redefining grace in terms of man's intangible soul, rather than its association with God. Nature became defined by mathematical and empirical sciences. Secular man thus began to view himself as an autonomous, "rational" being able to decide truth on his own. But in conflict with this was the rising view of life as purely mechanically predetermined.

How could man reason yet be purely mechanical? Raphael (1453-20) painted it, Da Vinci (1452-1519) struggled but failed to unite it. The reason: God must be in the equation.

In response or parallel to the Renaissance, the Reformation took place. It dealt with 2 primary issues according to Schaeffer: one, growing humanism in the Catholic Church, and two, the "incorrect" perception of Aquinas that man's fall did not affect his entire being (including the intellect). Some like Thomas More (1477-1535) tried to reform the church from within, others like Luther by leaving it. Calvin, Luther and others redefined the issues; man was completely depraved and fallen, only God was holy and good, and the scriptures were the final authority for knowledge. This affected how they viewed nature. It too was fallen, like man; yet man retained the imprint of God's image and thus man was different from the rest of nature. Art by Reformation artists was realistic but emphasized spiritual issues, e.g. Durer.

Modern science developed out of this period as men like Galileo, Kepler, Copernicus began to "think God's thoughts after Him" regarding the physical universe. There was a trust that the universe was orderly and had purpose, and as it was God's glory to "conceal a matter" it was king's obligation to seek it (Proverbs 25:2), for the "heavens declare the glory of God" (Psalm 19:1), and '"truth springs forth from the earth" (Psalm 80:11).

Schaeffer then notes that among secular man during the Enlightenment there arose the dichotomy of freedom/nature, as propounded by Kant (1724-1804), and Rousseau (1712-1778). Grace was removed as a concept, nature by being deterministic had devoured it. There was no need for sin or redemption. Thus as a rational being the individual was "free" to do whatever he desired. Man became increasingly centered on self-gratification. Yet this created considerable conflict with the scientific determinists in which freedom was predetermined and thus meaningless. Again, without God tangible and intangible unity was impossible. Pornography and other vices, which flourished in the Renaissance did so here as well. Benjamin Franklin, typical of this mindset, had a large pornographic collection.

While Rousseau promoted freedom, Hegel (1770-1831) promoted relativism. The idea of a thesis and antithesis, that is, a given view and its opposing view was rejected, there being only partial truth in each, thus one should "synthesize" them together and all becomes relative. Schaeffer says this represents man in rebellion against God, by placing himself at the center of the universe, deciding right from wrong; and since he lacks "all knowledge" his conclusions result in an ambivalent "grayness".

The next step in secular philosophy which affects man even today was the Existentialism of Kierkegaard (1813-1855), and Sartre (1905-1980). It implied a dichotomy of faith/rationality. Faith is not in God, but rather a nonrational optimism, in contrast to rationality which equals pessimism because naturalistic determinism had convinced people that there was no purpose to life. This philosophic system had and still does have religious and secular branches. Kierkegaard believed the Bible to have errors but held that it should be followed anyway. Sartre advocated a meaningless universe, and that one must "authenticate self" by an action of the will. Jasper talked about a final experience giving certainty that a person exists in the midst of meaninglessness. Aldous Huxley advocated the use of hallucinogens to get a "first order experience". The practical outplaying of this philosophy in secular science is the optimistic hope, without evidence, that a final proof for evolution will be found. Thus while many secular scientists disparage Christians for supposedly having blind optimism, they themselves practice it. (This will be discussed more in Chapter 4 Science.)

Schaeffer concludes that man's continual rejection of God's revealed word of wisdom and truth has lead to the present despondent determinism in conflict with an irrational optimism, and that true unity and perspective must come from understanding God and His purposes.

Since the time of writing of Schaeffer's books (1972, 1976) philosophic thinking has developed a step further. The pessimism created by naturalistic determinism is still present, but the irrational optimism is rejected. In its place is a void or acceptance of hedonistic pleasures. This is Nihilism. No absolutes are accepted, no morals, no religious precepts. Art like a burnt flag laying on the floor or a cross in urine reflects this period. Nihilism then leads to Anarchy, a revolt against established order. Nihilists have been present in every age, but in the present age they are more prevalent.

In stark contrast to this is the "End-Times" philosophy/theology propounded by Christian groups. Many believe

God is allowing secular man to reap the temporal consequences of godless philosophies. They acknowledge that mankind is in an increasingly precarious position, e.g. atomic and biologic weapon expansion and recurring natural disasters, famine, and endless new diseases. These Christians believe that God will bring His judgment against mankind to a culmination, called the Great Tribulation. After this period will occur a time of restoration of peace, justice, and righteousness, the Millennium. Thus Christians should have a true hope (expectation of good), based in a reasoned faith.

Below, certain philosophic systems, their history, tenets, and a Christian response will be reviewed.

The Classical Philosophers: Socrates, Plato, Aristotle

Background and Tenets

W. Durant, a secular historian of philosophy, states that philosophy covers 5 areas: logic, esthetics, ethics, politics, and metaphysics. Logic is the (study of) method of thought: observation, deduction, and hypothesis. Esthetics: study of form, i.e. beauty. Ethics: study of conduct. Politics: of social organization. Metaphysics: of ultimate reality or the interrelation of mind and matter (as a secularist he does not acknowledge the spirit).

The early classical philosophers often wrote regarding these areas. Yet Schaeffer states that they adhered to 3 tenets:

1) Man, by his mind alone, can gather information in particulars and develop general universal concepts.
2) Reality is rational; there is truth and untruth.
3) All knowledge can be unified; something that modem philosophers have rejected (as will be discussed).

Socrates, Plato, and Aristotle form the foundation of the early Greek philosophers. W. Sahakian remarks that Socrates (469-399 BC) emphasized knowing not only the extant environment but "thyself", and to have true insight (virtue, excellence, prudence, etc.) one had to be guided by an accurate understanding of both the material world and one's inner nature. This was gained by self examination. As reported by Plato, he developed an inductive form of inquiry, the "Socratic dialectic", that by patient questioning of a pupil the teacher could bring him to understand the correct conclusion. He felt that with accurate knowledge one will automatically do what is right. From doing right, good comes which results in happiness. He therefore thought the most educated should be the leaders of society.

Plato (428-348 BC) was a student of Socrates for 8 years. He promoted Socrates' style of teaching. He agreed with Socrates that acquisition of knowledge is necessary to pursue good, and that the willingness to do it was necessary as well. He then constructed a dualistic paradigm of a phenomenalistic (physical) world and an idealistic (intangible) one. The physical is an imperfect reflection of the perfect idea (or Form); this is his theory of Forms. God, who is perfect, created the physical world out of imperfect materials, resulting in its imperfection. Man's soul originated in the ideal world and returns to it after its temporary physical confinement. The goal of physical life is self-realization, by doing good and becoming more like God. Antony Flew states he, Plato, believed that all men seek to do good but act wrong only because of ignorance (imperfection) and that no wrongdoing is voluntary.

Political systems (his book *The Republic*) can be collectively good or evil. Sahakian comments that Plato believed that the good government results in an individual's attainment of his or her best abilities. It is lead by one or a few leaders. A poor one is the result of greed among the leaders and thus results in a lack of self-realization by individuals; yet he argued that "might makes right". Intelligence and courage are exalted, and justice is relative to the form of government. A timocracy (rule by one person) is of a higher form than the oligarchy (rule by a few wealthy individuals), then a democracy (government by the masses), and finally lowest, a tyranny (an individual rules for sake of his unjust interests). In emphasizing free will he noted any government may perish by excess of its basic concept. Timocracy might lead to tyranny, oligarchy to greedy gain of the few, and democracy to mob rule.

In The Republic education is available to all, and Plato even argued for children to be removed from parents so as to get proper training (i.e. each child as a "clean slate" is to be given equal opportunity). Positions in society are then based upon the individual's resulting skills. Those skilled in wisdom (guardians) were to be given ruling positions, those of courage (valor) as warriors to defend the state, and the masses of artisans to manufacture material goods according to the needs of the state.

Aristotle (384-322 BC) studied with Plato for 20 years. He subsequently taught Alexander the Great. He has been called the "founder of science" but not of empiricism (the physical testing of ideas). He felt that all truth could be obtained through reasoning and simple observation. He defined truth as a correct assessment of the real world. He developed syllogisms, i.e. that a conclusion follows from connected precepts. Examples include deduction from a general principle to a particular event or thing and induction from the particular to the general. He did not attempt the process of empirical verification. Aristotle was particularly interested in the relationship of the form (essence) of something and its composition or matter (substance) as Plato before him; although to Plato the true essence of something was immaterial and to Aristotle it was only material. He felt that function demanded a form; if there was not a function, then matter would be chaotic and without shape. He felt one could by "reason" discover the relationship. Aristotle felt there were four forces that affected matter: 1) matter itself, 2) form (function of the matter), 3) motion (physical forces affecting the matter), and 4) the end purpose. Sahakian gives Aristotle's example of a bronze statue: made with bronze (matter) formed by an anvil (motion), into a shape, with a resultant purpose or end. In his view nature is thus imperfect but is forming into the perfect. The inorganic world is most imperfect, then the plant and animal kingdom, man, and finally God is perfect and without physical form. To Aristotle God is transcendent to the physical universe and is its creator. Thus He creates or causes its form and function.

Aristotle divided man into a physical and soulish being, the soul being immortal (exsisting before birth and after death). The soul, which cannot be actuated without the body, has two compartments; the first involves the human mind and sensual input. It is passive, a blank tablet, upon which are written experiences. The second involves the will and ability to reason. These ideas have permeated psychiatric concepts even unto the current day. He considered goodness attaining one's "potential", with the process of reasoning being the highest. By it an individual achieves self discipline, not too much and not too little.

He wrote much on ethics. Virtues are human activities such as temperance, liberality, honor, gentleness, friendliness, truthfulness, etc. that require reason and an act of the will. He felt that by practicing these one would lead a peaceful orderly life. In contrast if one practiced vices (the opposite to virtues) conflicts would occur.

Aristotle's views on personal ethics affected his views on societal ones as well. As Sahakian has commented, it was Aristotle's view that the purpose of state government was to raise individuals from a "crude natural condition'" to that of a more "civilized culture" which included instruction in the use of the arts (grammar, logic) and the sciences. This training was to benefit the individual and the state. He felt that a society was necessary for man to develop, and that man's nature was one of peace; thus society could develop in peace.

He preferred the monarchy as the best form of government, then aristocracy (rule by the best citizens), then polity (rule by the masses). Monarchy could corrupt to tyranny, aristocracy to an oligarchy, and polity to a democracy, a rule in which each is only interested in his own gain. He felt women, children, and slaves should be excluded from the government, but that children should be educated.

Aristotle had a profound impact on science, religion, and social ethics in his time which has reverberated even into our present age.

Christian Teachings and Approaches to Evangelism

When one reviews the classical philosophers it is easy to be impressed by their struggles to understand the questions of life. Yet it should be remembered that probably all had been exposed to the Old Testament scriptures, i.e. the Pentateuch. Plato traveled through the Middle East for several years and must have heard of the Jewish religion. In fact, early Christian writers like Justin Martyr (100 AD) assumed that many of Plato's concepts of God came from them, and were then corrupted by his own ideas. Why, as Mohammed after them, did they not respond to the Jewish scriptures? One problem is that Jews often failed to evangelize the cultures around them, but the second more important reason is probably that most philosophers were "wise in their own eyes". Virtually all the philosophic systems throughout history are alternative explanations to the views of the Bible. They simply did not accept or lacked a knowledge of what God had revealed.

For example, in their "Tragedies" they would write about man's pride and evil nature, but they had no real concept of God's deliverance and redemption from sin. To them the goal of life was attempting to do good, whereby one becomes more perfected, like God. Isaiah 64:6 says all of man's works are as dirty rags to God. We can only have good works by confessing sins to God, receiving His forgiveness and then obeying His word. The subtle difference is that in the first case a man, by himself, improves, perfects, and purifies himself; and in the second God does it through a man. In the first glory belongs to man and in the second to God.

Because these philosophers did not understand sin, their views of government and ethics were distorted. They presented government as a necessary instrument (which it is), but concluded that it was often useful in teaching morals and behavior to the masses by a few select individuals. Monarchy and aristocracy were favored. The emphasis was placed on the ability of a few benevolent, capable leaders to instruct the many. Education of the young, even by separating them from their parents (Plato's advice), was seen as essential to this process. Training depended one's capabilities, and what was good for society was good for the individual. While the potential for "evil" leadership was acknowledged, the idea of a pervasive sin-nature among all men was largely ignored. Yet, the Bible clearly teaches that all men are corrupted (Psalm 51:5 and Psalm 14:1-3). One aspect of this nature that can be seen in men throughout history is greed. As the scriptures say the love of money is a root of evil. These philosophers seem willfully ignorant of this. While one could argue whether a democracy is a good or bad form of government, some of the founding fathers of the U.S. Constitution did believe in the depravity of man and his need for God's guidance. Thus, they formed a republic (a representative government) and attempted to divide the functions of government into separate subgroups. They regularly sought God in prayer and fasting. Israel's God-given form was a theocracy, with the Biblical scriptures as the basis of authority. However, many others were influenced by the secular philosophies.

Finally, these philosophers' perception of God was vague and ill-defined. He was not the majestic, holy, personal God of the Pentateuch. As Christians and as ambassadors for Christ, we can offer people a personal relationship with the creator God, who desires to be a Father to them.

Rationalism

Background

Rene Descartes (1596-1650), and Benedict Spinoza (1632-1677) were prominent Rationalist philosophers. Their works during the late "Renaissance" led directly to those of the "Enlightenment" of Rousseau and Kant. The pivot point of all Rationalists was the belief that man is able to discover knowledge and truth by reason alone, and that it is superior to sense perception or conscience and can proceed along lines of precepts. As Descartes said, "I think therefore I am." They also attempted to unify all knowledge gathered from reason and experience. In this they re-invigorated what the classical philosophers held. Descartes and Spinoza attempted to unify it in mathematical terms. Spinoza wrote, "I will write about human beings as though I were concerned with lines and planes and solids." They talked about the universe as having fixed immutable laws, ordained by God, in which man and all other life forms have an existence. In this the will of man was subjugated to a type of determinism; and while to Descartes God was outside of nature (part of his dualism of mind/matter), to Spinoza God was within all nature (pantheism). Jesus Christ was only considered a great teacher. Other rationalists did not accept the concept of God, and proposed to order the universe by naturalistic principles alone.

Most agreed virtue is knowledge. "To understand is the first and only basis of virtue," said Spinoza. By reasoned use of it the passions of man could be restrained. He, in his system of ethics, stated that all men act out of self-preservation, and thus would gather together for mutual self-defense. Leaders of these groups should, in desirable circumstances, be those who are of the highest "virtues".

In the coming years the Rationalists were supplanted by the Empiricists or Naturalists, who held that sensory perception had the pre-eminent effect on a person's thinking (John Locke, David Hume). Yet, Spinoza's concept of self-preservation did influence Nitzsche (who advocated the "will to power"), and his pantheism sustained Hegel.

Tenets

1) Reason is sufficient to understand truth.
2) Truth is self-evident, deductive in character.

3) The physical and non-physical universe is governed by a single system of laws e.g., that can be described by mathematics.

4) To some, belief in God is based in a fait which is irrational therefore He does not exists. To others, God exists and unifies everything by immutable laws. Thus, to Spinoza, He is part of nature; to Descartes, He is outside of it. But to both, He is impersonal and Jesus Christ as divine is an irrational concept, and is therefore not accepted.

5) Sin does not exist. To some, the will is nonexistent; to others it is limited.

6) The highest virtue is knowledge, and by reasoned use of knowledge passions are controlled. Political leaders should be those of highest "virtues".

Christian Teachings and Approaches to Evangelism

1) The basic misconception is the rejection of sin by the Rational philosophers. In doing so they deny that the intellect can be distorted, and thus they deny their dependence on God for truth. Jonathan Edwards (1758) contested this view when he said the "state of man's nature , that disposition of the mind, is to be looked upon as evil and pernicious, were it not the free mercy and kindness of God interposes ..." These philosophers fell for the same temptation Eve experienced in the Garden; "hath God said" or rather "you can know the truth apart from God". Christians need to stand firm that God's word regarding sin and its consequences is true. (See Proverbs 14:12, 16:25, 3:5)

2) Spinoza extensively studied the scriptures but denied many of the principles such as the deity of Christ, called angels hallucinations, rejected the concept of free will, and sin, and thought that God was material, part of nature.

3) The fruit of Rationalism did not lead to a unity of knowledge nor peace or good but rather to corruption as Schaeffer has well documented.

4) The Christian should avoid the trap that unregenerate men fall into, and follow Watchman Nee's admonition to let God's Spirit guide them in the acquisition and use of knowledge. A truthful Christian witness and life is what most rationalists need to see.

Naturalism (Positivism)

Background

Naturalism or positivism (the term used in the 1800's) was further defined according to Comte as "the whole body of human knowledge. Human knowledge is the result of the study of the forces belonging to matter, and of the conditions or laws governing those forces." In other words, there is nothing of relevance outside of the physical realm. This *a priori* assumption was not new with Comte. Hume propounded it in the 1700's (limiting it to sense knowledge) and even among the Greeks it was a common view. The Ionian philosophers such as Democritus (460-360 BC) stated, "in reality there are only atoms and the void"; there is no purpose or design only matter, form, and being destroyed in chaos. Many, such as Empedocles (445 BC) advocated organisms arising spontaneously and over time changing (evolving) into other forms, called the Great Chain of Being. Heraclitus (530-470 BC) stated that life was a cycle begun with fire and driven by strife. Durant summarizes their world view as, "Perception is due to the expulsion of atoms from the object upon the sense organ. There is or have been or will be an infinite number of worlds; at every moment planets are colliding and dying, and new worlds are rising out of chaos by the selective aggregation of atoms of similar size and shape. There is no design; the universe is a machine." (It should be noted that out of this view came little true empirical science or development of technology.) Lucretius (95-55 BC) consolidated these views in a treatise, *On the Nature of Things*, in which he expounded on a mechanistic origin and purpose for the universe.

Comte's positivism was popularized by Charles Darwin. In 1859 his *Origin of the Species* gave a superficial account of how life could have possibly been transformed from one life form to another without miraculous intervention; yet he never actually showed it to occur. He was well received. Hoyle has commented that the reason Darwin's book became popular is that it "broke the tyranny of Christianity over people". In the latter part of the 1800's the implications of naturalism (and its exclusion of God) were again (like in Greece) expanded to the humanities, e.g. law, education, ethics by Herbert Spencer (father of modern sociology), John Dewey (father of government education), and Francis Galton (Darwin's first cousin and a founder of eugenics, the process of improving the human race by selection). Hitler, Mao, and Stalin utilized their ideas to carry out genocides. Today, Peter Singer, ethicist, argues it is morally better to use "defective humans" than "healthy" rats for biological experimentation. Planned Parenthood continues as the thriving offspring of the Eugenics Movement. Bertrand Russell, in the twentieth century, even pronounced that as man, through science, has harnessed the physical environment, so he will harness the "formation of human character." Many of the current colleges and universities remain dominated by naturalistic programs.

Tenets
1) The only reality is physical (Hume limits it to sensual perception alone).
2) Since most concepts of God state He is spiritual; God is largely excluded (except for pantheistic views, i.e. God is nature).
3) Corollary: there is no purposeful design. Religion or a belief in the supernatural is at best a deception and worse a fraud.
4) All truth, all meaning to life is to be found in studying nature.
5) Man using observation and reason can discover all truth.

Christian Teaching and Approach to Evangelism
1) Christians accept the teaching that there is a supernatural, and that man is not just flesh. There is good reason for this although it cannot be proven by simple physical measurements. The concept of causality argues for God, for we do see order and design in nature, contrary to much naturalistic thinking. For example, all of man's creative inventions employ principles and concepts already inherent in nature, e.g. the computer is similar to the brain, the camera to an eye, a pump to the heart, etc. While some philosophers like Hume argued against cause and effect, they were wrong. The Bible says in Romans 1:20, that the divine attributes and powers of God are made manifest to all men through the creation so that they are without excuse (in terms of knowing God). Affirming this in his time, John Calvin stated, "As the celebrated Cicero observes, there is no nation so barbarous, no race so savage as not to be firmly persuaded of the existence of God."

2) All truth cannot be contained in nature and natural physical

laws alone. For as Phillip Johnson states, "If science produces a universal law for everything then how can reasoning trusted, since all is reduced to a self propelling materialism? All is self-referred." In other words, if we are simply organic masses activated by atom particles bouncing off our bodily sensors (as the Greeks and modern reductionists believed), what use is reason; or even what is it?

Yet Natural law, according to Thomas Aquinas, and summarized by Charles Price is "a rule of reason, promulgated by God in man's nature, whereby man can discern how he should act." It requires one to believe in God.

In this the Christian has a great comfort. The Bible tells him that the Almighty Creator will send His Spirit who will guide the believer into all truth. We are not as Pilate saying, "What is truth?". We can study nature, philosophy, and religion and trust God to guide us into truth. The only caveat is we must want to know Him and be willing to obey Him; for whosoever walks in "the light comes to Him", and "all who call upon the name of the Lord will be saved".

3) Certain aspects of naturalism are not all bad. The emphasis on empiricism, or the actual physical testing of hypotheses (see Chapter 4 Science), is useful and freed science from many of the wrong concepts of Aristotle (who conjectured but never really tested). Yet it is presumption to exclude the supernatural. Man simply does not have all knowledge. Interestingly, Christians played a prominent role in the development of the Scientific Method.

4) Evangelism of a committed naturalist can be difficult, for they have fallen prey to the pride of intellectualism. In some cases discussing the fallacy of excluding the supernatural is useful. In others the weaknesses and lack of empirical data for evolution can help. Still for others the logical moral implications of naturalism and evolution i.e. abortion, eugenics/racism can turn the mind and heart. Others just need the faithful witness of an honest, hardworking, kind yet truthful relative or associate.

Existentialism

Background

The current ideas of existentialism had their roots in the writings of the Danish theologian/philosopher Soren Kierkegaard

(1813-1855). His writings have been secularized by Jean-Paul Sartre (1905-1980). W. Kaufmann states that these authors and others were in a sense rebelling against the onward march of mechanistic naturalism. Schaeffer describes their views as a dualism of mechanistic determinism and irrational optimism.

To Kierkegaard reality was to be based upon one's experience; it was not predetermined nor reason-based, "The mode of apprehension of the truth is precisely the truth." Sahakian states that Kierkegaard felt that man could develop through three stages of life: 1) aesthetic: a sensual uncommitted existence, 2) ethical: where experience resulted in morally committed decisions, and 3) religious: experience based upon commitment to God. Sartre rejected the third step stating that there is no reality beyond subjective experience. Yet he stated that it was man's desire to be a "god", that is, to be the final judge. He said man is "condemned to be free" since he must determine the reality of the world. He created a dualism of despair, by a sense of purposelessness, and yet of optimism that man, by sensual experiences, could direct his life.

Camus' novel *The Plague* (1947), reflects well the dualism of determinism/irrational optimism. The story involves a physician who attempts to bring healing to plague victims, knowing he will fail. This is similar to the concept of a man rolling a massive rock up an infinite hill, knowing that eventually he will tire out and the stone will crush him.

Tenets

1) Reality is to be tested by one's own subjective experiences.
2) There is no predetermined place or purpose for the individual; man cannot reason to understand his environment because it is not rational (in contrast to what the classical philosophers felt). To some it (the universe) is driven by a directionless mechanism.
3) Moral life is an illusion.
4) To remain authentic to oneself, one needs to resist the influences of society.

Christian Teachings and Approaches to Evangelism

This is a troubling philosophy to the Christian. It is introverted and very self-centered. Rational debate is probably not useful, as these people hold truth is relative to the eyes of the beholder. Each does what is wise in his own mind. This is a true antecedent of nihilism and anarchy. Possibly, concrete examples of cause and effect may help, e.g. heavy drinking leads to liver cirrhosis, break-up of the families, and motor vehicle accidents. Yet, people are not predestined to do these things. Prayer and the example of a steadfast holy life dedicated to God is important as well in witnessing to these people.

Christian Philosophy

Background

Christian philosophy starts with the premises: 1) God is the first cause, "I am that I am," 2) that truth (knowledge) exists, 3) God by His Spirit is willing to reveal truth to man, as He says, "Come let us reason together" (Isaiah 1:18; In this form of reasoning God convicts of His truth. He is the teacher.), and 4) man by studying all things and holding fast to that which is good, i.e., consistent with God's word, can know truth.

The Early Church father Justin Martyr (100-165 AD) was emphatic that true philosophic principles were to be found initially in the Jewish scriptures, that these were antecedent to any other sources. The unity that the classical philosophers looked for were to be found in them. God as creator, outside of the creation, holds mind and matter together. He is the one who assures us that we can reason, sense/feel; for without Him there is no guarantee of reality. As Anselm (1033 AD) has said, "the very thought that we conceive or think of God proves He exists." Thus the Christian has a reasoned hope as regards the gospel concepts of sin, judgment, eternal life, moral conduct, etc. Of all people the Christians have a reasoned understanding of why nations continually war against each other, why people lie, steal, and cheat. The Bible also gives them principles of conduct on how to live – e.g. Ten Commandments.

The concepts of facts, knowledge, understanding, and wisdom must be applied within the setting of a belief in God. For in Proverbs it says that the "fear of the Lord is the beginning of wisdom." One cannot know the fuller context of the issues of life without knowing God's will and desires. Secular man can apply these principles, with limited success to the physical realm, but the spiritually minded

Christian applies then to the eternal goals of God. The secular man may build a temporary earthly company, but the godly person builds an eternal home (Psalm 127:1-2). The Christian is to diligently study and learn facts. He is to understand them within the context of scripture, and then to apply them (wisdom) as guided by God's Spirit. For example, a scientist, who is a Christian, can learn the scientific method and observe events (or facts). By this he begins to understand how they reveal God as the creator. He then applies his knowledge to the healing arts of medicine or other beneficial activities and in a timely manner he shares God's plan for man with a secular associate with the hope of that person gaining eternal salvation. His impact is both temporal and eternal.

Through the last 6000 years nothing new (as a philosophic principle of life) has been thought by man that has not already been reasoned before, as Solomon said. Mankind in each generation has been presented with the evidence of a created universe, and thus a creator (more powerful than man), the awareness of the corruption of his behavior (by an internal conscience), and the need of God to intervene. Each man, woman, and child in each age is presented with the precise influence to bring them to the point of "what will you do with God?" Even those who have not heard the gospel are judged by their own consciences (Romans 2:14-15) and the witness of God's Holy Spirit. Thus no man will be able to say to God, "You did not give me reasonable evidence of yourself." We as Christians must beseech men to be reconciled to God, as their reasonable service to Him the Almighty Creator.

As Christian philosophers have combated false philosophies and heresies through the ages, the fundamentals have not changed, for God is the Alpha and Omega. He knows man's condition and the eternal principles to be applied. At various times certain Godly principles have been given pre-eminence according to the need of the moment. Early in the church history false concepts of Christ's divinity and humanity were clarified by various creeds such as the Nicene Creed. Later as man began to exalt human experience and knowledge leaders like Calvin boldly asserted that man was completely corrupted spirit, soul, mind, and body; so that man needed to be renovated in all these areas by God's Spirit and Word. With the development of Naturalism and its logical social consequences like racism, genocide, and immorality, men like Butler,

Wilberforce, Finney and others called men to reject the false philosophies and repent. Unfortunately, there has been a progressive slide of the bulk of mankind away from repentance and obedience to God, as it is written, "The way is broad that leads to destruction, and many are those who enter by it. For the gate is small and the way is narrow that leads to life, and few are those who find it." (Matthew 7:13-14) Yet God is not a respecter of persons, and all who call upon His Name shall be saved. Therefore, Christians are to cry out to those around them to be reasonable and repent.

Tenets
1) There is a creator; we see the orderly designed universe and cause and effect argues for a designer/creator.
2) Because there is a creator there is absolute truth, but man as a finite being can only know truth as God teaches him. God is willing to do this.
3) Man is a triune being: spirit, soul, and body. God is a triune being and interacts with man at every facet of his being.
4) The concept of sin is true, because God has determined right and wrong behavior, e.g. ten commandments. God has given man the ability to obey or disobey, but the consequences are preset. Christ paid the penalty for sin so man could choose to accept or reject this forgiveness.
5) There is a final judgment where God judges the conduct of each person and man receives eternal rewards or punishment.

Christian Teachings and Apologetics
See Christian Philosophy.

Conclusion

In reviewing different philosophers, the first division takes place as to whether God or man is "the measure of all things". The secular philosopher states that the human mind is the final judge of reality, right/wrong, and ultimate arbiter of the purpose of life. The Bible teaches that men's minds are corrupted and that all men are born into, and commit sin; that is, all men are rebellious to the purposes of God. As such man cannot know truth or "purify" himself by his own efforts. Only God can teach man truth and "purify" him. All the secular philosophers discussed and rejected the concept of sin. Yet by experiencing the truth of God's Word and His goodness, man will often convert to God's view. This is a true miracle and mystery: what causes a man to lose his self-exalted life to gain a submitted life in Christ?

In the midst of man's rebellion and denial of His obvious presence, God still reveals Himself to mankind. His creation, the intricate interworkings of nature, proclaim Him (Romans 1) in a general sense. His written word, carefully delivered to men over several centuries, reflects His personal attributes, and man's relationship to Him. All men have a knowledge of God.

To those who reject God's Spirit, there can only be confusion and error. The bulk of philosophic systems fall into this darkness. The writers such as Hume, Comte, and others pridefully attempted to redefine reality in terms acceptable to themselves. Thus, for anyone to coherently discuss their system they must converse in their terms; and the philosopher becomes a god who has created his own world system. Each of these systems found ways to appease the natural mind. The Rationalists reasoned reality in their minds; Descartes used math as his language. The Naturalists talked in terms of genetic predestination. Existentialists were committed to licentious sense experience alone. Many claimed to include God in their construct, and in doing so they claimed to understand God, but they usually denied the power of His Word (the Bible) to change lives.

The Bible says not to be taken captive by the philosophy and empty deception of men (Colossians 2:8). God desires man to understand who He is and man's relationship to God. Romans 1:18-32 describes the downward spiral of rejecting His truth. (See **Figure 6**)

FIGURE 6

The Progression of Secular Philosophy Through the Ages
In Confirmation of Romans 1:18-32

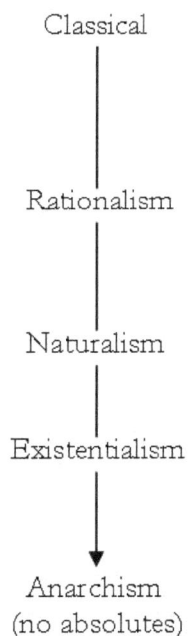

Secular Philosophy	Attitude of Individual
Classical	universe has logical principles; God exists though impersonal
Rationalism	redefine or deny God/ false wisdom exalt intellect
Naturalism	worship nature
Existentialism	hedonism (lusts of the flesh) worship of self
Anarchism (no absolutes)	approve those who practice evil deeds

It should be noted that the general characteristics of each of these philosophic systems have occurred simultaneously throughout time. (See **Figure 7**) Their popularity has ebbed and flowed depending on the popularity of a given proponent. Ecclesiastes says there is nothing new under the sun. Shaeffer says that the modern trend away from Biblical concepts occurred with Aquinas. Hilaire Belloc (French Catholic historian) says it occurred during the Reformation.

In any case, there has been an inexorable trend in deterioration of general philosophic systems away from Biblical precepts.

As was noted in the overview, accurate reasoning involves several premises (or primary assumptions):

1) 1) That truth can be discovered. Many modern philosophers deny this; Pilate's question, "What is truth," is indicative of secular relativism. But the Bible says God's Spirit will guide all who call upon Him into truth.

2) That reality is real. Many modern philosophers deny this. The Bible says God has revealed Himself to all men through the creation (Romans 1); for example, the stars declare the glory of God, and truth springs forth from the earth (Psalm 19:1; 85:11).

3) As man has a finite capacity for knowledge and understanding - he has a limited grasp of truth.

The Bible teaches that mankind has been able to reason since the Garden of Eden. For it is there that Satan appeared to Eve and said, "Has God said?" He then went on to say, "That in the day you eat from it your eyes will be opened and you will be like God, knowing good and evil." (Genesis 3: 1, 5) The fall of man's mind and his ability to accurately reason fell at the moment of Eve's and Adam's eating the apple. For they attempted to acquire knowledge separately from God's spiritual guidance.

Yet, it is important for man to reason and to collect facts from various sources before making judgment on an issue. The Bible says, "Examine everything; hold fast to that which is good," 1 Thessalonians 5:21. But he must have the guidance of God's Spirit and Word. Without this influence, man's understanding of truth remains relative, as no man knows all so as to put truth in context. Benjamin Rush (founder of Psychiatry in America) stated that for American youth to become law abiding, responsible citizens they needed training in the scriptures, even in public school.

Therefore, Christians are able to boldly pursue knowledge, as the early theologians and scientists did, because they have great confidence that God's Spirit will guide them into all truth. Those who reject God's guidance do not have this assurance, and walk in darkness, despair, and destruction.

The Christian needs to be "wise as a serpent, and innocent as a dove." It is useful to have a cursory knowledge of what secular philosophers have taught, so as to understand secular thinking, but not to be beguiled by them. On the other hand, to reason in light of God's Word is a great adventure.

FIGURE 7

Judeo/Christian
Period   Judeo/Christian Roots ⟶

Time   (4000 BC – 400 AD)

Writers   Apostles
                  Prophets
                  Early Church Fathers – Augustine, Justin Martyr

Dichotomy   God
                     Man
                  animal/plant/earth

Character   God Creator
                  Man created in God's image but now fallen
                  Man composed of spirit, soul, body
                  10 commandments basis of morality
                  Truth is God's revealed Word
                  Unity of spiritual, soulish, and earthly in God

Secular
Period   Classical ⟶
                                   Atomist
Time   (400-300 BC)   (500-50 BC)

Writers   Socrates   Democritus
                  Plato   Empedocles
                  Aristotle

Dichotomy   mind = unity   matter only
                  Matter

Character   rational – man capable of gathering particulars
                          to form universal principles
                          - that there is truth and untruth
                  unity – possible of all knowledge
                  god – as an entity by some; no god or spirit realm by others

Judeo-Christian

Period	Byzantine ──────────────────────────────▶	
Time	(400- 1225)	
Writers		**Aquinas** (1225-1274)
Dichotomy	Heavenly Earthly	Grace Nature
Character	Nature less important than spiritual Art – symbolic representation of heaven, nature ignored	Nature put on equal footing with spiritual Sin did not affect intellect Art – realism nature more emphasized

Secular
Period ──────────────────────────────▶

Judeo/Christian

Period	<u>Reformation</u> ⟶
Time	(1517-1648)
Writers	Luther Protestant Calvin T. Moore Catholic Bacon
Dichotomy	<u>God</u> Man animals/plants/earth
Character	Spiritual reemphasized with God as Creator Man viewed as completely fallen along with nature Art – realism but with spiritual emphasis – (Durer) Modern science had roots in

Secular

Period	<u>Renaissance</u> ⟶
Time	(1300-1600)
Writers	Petrarch/Machiavelli Hobbes/DaVinci
Dichotomy	<u>universal – grace</u> particular – nature
Character	Spiritual excludes God, reflects man's intellectual capabilities – humanism Naturalism – renewal of nature viewed as mechanical Art – pornography

Judeo/Christian

Period	Revival ⟶ Social Gospel ⟶
Time	(1648-1789) / (1789-1900)

Period Revival ⟶ Social Gospel ⟶

Time (1648-1789)   (1789-1900)

Writers
J. Edwards	Finney/Paley
Whitfield	Butler
Wesley/ Newton	Wilberforce/ Beattie

Dichotomy
God
Man

Character

Bible inerrant	Biblical principles relevant to society
Sin/repentance	*Abolition of English slave trade
Life after death	*Reform child labor law
God creator	Rejection of determinism/evolution
Puritan work ethic	Reemphasis on empirical
Moral absolutes	Data obtained by scientific method
	Causality, design

Secular

Period Enlightenment ⟶ Socialism ⟶

Time (1600-1800)   (1800-1900)

Writers
Kant/Rousseau	Hegel
Voltaire/Hume	Darwin
Descartes/Spinoza	Spencer

Dichotomy
Freedom	Thesis + Antithesis = Synthesis
Nature	

Character

God, grace rejected	No absolutes, all relative
Autonomy of individual	becomes more popular
emphasized = Freedom	Naturalism emphasized
Nature still deterministic	Evolution popularized:
in conflict with freedom	biologic, social application
Art – more abstract;	
pornographic;	
nature prominent	
Rationalism – reason exalted	

Judeo/Christian
Period ————————▶ Missions ————————————▶

Time   (1800-present)

Writers   H. Taylor/ W. Carey
                                Livingstone

Dichotomy   God
                                man

Character   Inerrancy of Bible
                                Going into all the earth
                                Signs & wonders confirm gospel

          Higher Criticism
          (secularized theology)
          (late 1800's)
          Wellhausen
          faith – irrational   Kierkegaard
          reason – rational   Bible has errors but must be followed
          Bible collection of human
          documents regarding God
Secular
Period ————————▶ Existentialism ————————————▶

Time   (1900-present)

Writers   Sartre

Dichotomy   Irrational optimism
                                Natural pessimism

Character   Emphasis of sensual experience
                                Optimistic by choice of will
                                Pessimistic because of naturalistic
                                  determinism creates conflict

Judeo/Christian

Period	End Time Revival
Time	(present)
Writers	B. Graham L. Palau Promise Keepers
Dichotomy	God man
Character	Judgment and destruction of present earth with new world to follow for those who obey God God's provision in difficult times Evangelism – global

Secular

Period	Nihilism/Anarchism
Time	(present)
Writers	Sagan, Pinker
Dichotomy	Hedonism Pessimism
Character	No boundaries; seek pleasure Art – reflects rebellion against any authority Postmodernism No accountability as all is reduced in severe reductionism to "My genes made me do it"

CHAPTER 4

SCIENCE

Introduction - What Science Is and What It Can Answer

Science as a general concept involves the systematic study and organization of groups of information. In a practical sense and in common usage it is simply the observation of the physical universe. By this definition, it can be used to ask only two basic types of questions: 1) classification: for example, "what is its color", "how heavy is it", etc. and, 2) directly observed change: for example, "will heating/cooling alter it?" In neither way can it answer aesthetic questions, e.g. is something beautiful, or definitively answer questions regarding future or past events outside of recorded human observations. But it can be applied in technology to manipulate and utilize the physical environs in which we live. Many well-known authors have spent hundreds of pages attempting to answer what is science, but this difficulty often arises because of an over-reaching view of science into religion and philosophy.

Science interfaces into philosophy when one considers concepts such as induction, deduction, reduction, and religion when it is used to support claims regarding ultimate causes and purposes.

Definitions

Science: to observe nature. Each person in a way can and does practice science. Jean Fabre used to take his students on a field trip, then asked them to observe and describe what they saw in one square foot of field. As such the students could have addressed two types of questions: 1) classification - descriptions of objects and grouping of them by physical characteristics e.g. color, height, weight, etc.; and 2) changes in the properties of substances under differing conditions or time, e.g. what happens when a candle burns a leaf? J.B. Conant adds that true science involves conceiving new concepts and not just new ways of aggregating data. He lumps what are called social sciences (archeology, anthropology, etc.) into the social philosophies, even though at times they may use certain methodologies developed by the sciences. While philosophy addresses ethical and moral questions, it is certain that science cannot. Nor can it give an understanding as to why something is. "Why" implies understanding a motive. Science can be used to describe what, where, and when only.

Induction: a process of logic whereby in observing the characteristics of an individual object a general statement is made about others not yet observed, but which may occur fully within the same conditions and categories. For example, several captured flies have four wings, therefore it is assumed all flies have four wings. The weakness of this logic of course is that without observing every fly that exists, it isn't known if the statement is completely true.

Deduction: a process of logic whereby a general statement is tested by observing individual application of it. For example, if it is assumed all flies have four wings, a recently caught insect can be considered a fly only if it has four wings. The weakness in this logic is that unexpected observations may be discarded, when the general statement is assumed to be always true.

Reduction: a process of logic whereby a complete complex structure is reduced to its simplest components, with the desired result that if individual simple components are analyzed and understood these can be extrapolated to the full complex structure. The weakness in this logic, is that something may be reduced so far as to make it unrecognizable as a part of the complex structure, e.g., breaking a computer apart into its individual wires, bolts, and nuts that could belong to any electrical instrument.

Scientific method: It involves a collection of observations developed into a hypothesis, applied by induction to form a theory. The theory is then tested by the deduction to predict certain results and is verified by observation whether these occur or not. The theory should be supported, modified, or discarded based on the results (see Scientific Method section).

The Scientific Method

The scientific method currently used was developed in the setting of the Christian worldview. This is because it required certain assumptions:

1) ethical norms; honesty is essential.
2) personal power of the scientist: mental capability, equipment, etc.
3) validity of laws of logic: that reality is, that there are laws of nature, and they are reproducible, etc.
4) confirmatory testing of others, as all scientists are affected by bias and limited by understanding of observations.

Its key elements are composed of 1) observations, 2) hypothesis, 3) theory, 4) law, (see **Figure 8**, "The Scientific Method").

Observation: involves watching an event, a fact. Yet it can become very complicated. In the present-day, sophisticated machinery is often required to detect extremely small particles and short time intervals. Thus, the reliability of the testing equipment itself must be tested and calibrated. This can be expensive, limiting the scope of experimentation that a scientist may perform. Most experiments are actually the testing of small extrapolations of prior known information, and in this sense knowledge is collected "bit by bit". How this knowledge is perceived, what emphasis is placed on it, how it guides further experimentation is affected by the scientist's overall views, his skill, etc. Scientists are very much driven by "consensus opinion" of colleagues. Thus most scientific observation and discovery proceeds at a "snail's pace". Any aberrant observations or ideas are usually, at least initially, resisted. Also, observation ends up being only an approximation of reality and may be compatible with many paradigms (world views), thus while data may be collected by accretion, the interpretations of it often proceeds by revolutions (overthrow of previous hypotheses or theories). Concepts regarding light are good examples; it was first considered a particle, then a wave, and now a photon.

Hypothesis/Theory: A hypothesis is a preliminary postulate attempting to explain a few observations. A theory is simply based on more observations. J. G. Kemeny differentiates between a fact and a hypothesis and theory in that the latter also involves speculation about events not yet observed and the former is a given, observed event. When looking at a number of plausible hypotheses for a given set of observations, generally the simplest, most reasonable one is accepted, Occam's Razor. However, given the biased nature of man, one may be accepted because of preconceptions of the scientist(s).

Many hypotheses or theories are derived from variations in observations under given conditions. The Null hypothesis questions whether these variations are simply due to sampling errors. An example would be that the observed mean length of survival of certain cancer patients treated with a chemical agent is five years vs. 4.8 years without treatment. If the overlap of the distribution of these two groups is more than five percent (convention dictates significance levels of five percent or one percent overlap), the treatment group would be, by convention, not significantly different from the untreated group and the Null hypothesis would be accepted. Statistics, especially those of "closer approximations", play an important part in the interpretation or theorizing of experimental results.

Law: a theory becomes a law when tested repeatedly under given conditions, and in which the observations are consistently confirmed. Because these laws are man-made, they can in the course of time be overturned by more relevant and accurate ones.

The scientific method is not foolproof, but it is a useful technique for qualitative and quantitative assessment of our physical environment in an orderly fashion. Yet it only approximates reality. Thus while the principles of God are absolute, and his order in design of the universe is unchanging, man's perception of it is continually being revised.

FIGURE 8

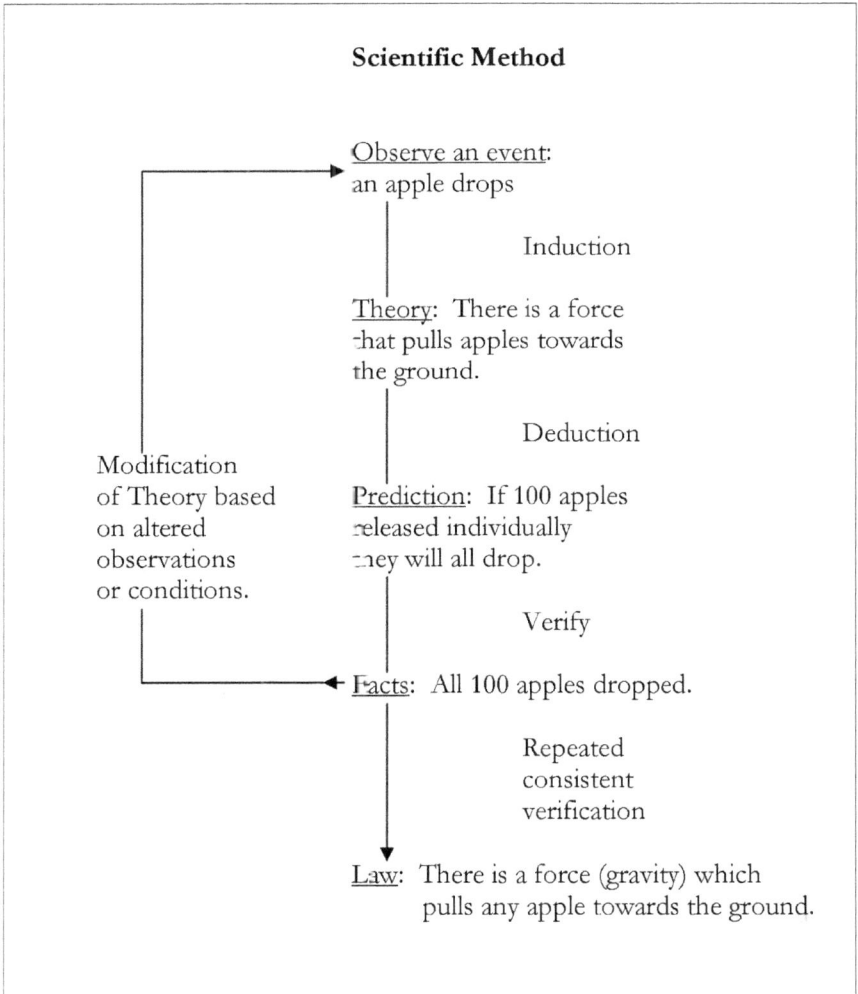

Scientific Method

Observe an event: an apple drops

Induction

Theory: There is a force that pulls apples towards the ground.

Deduction

Modification of Theory based on altered observations or conditions.

Prediction: If 100 apples released individually they will all drop.

Verify

Facts: All 100 apples dropped.

Repeated consistent verification

Law: There is a force (gravity) which pulls any apple towards the ground.

Pasteur's experiments, in the mid-1800's, disproving spontaneous generation are a good example of the application of the scientific method to a problem. It was noted that broth left open to air quickly spoiled. This was a problem for the food industry. Pasteur hypothesized that there were microscopic life forms found in the air that caused the spoiling upon settling and growing in the food. He felt that they did not arise by spontaneous development in the meat broth. He further hypothesized that heating would kill any of these life forms already in the broth, and that by sealing it from exposure to air he would block any further contamination. To test this, he boiled broths in glass flasks. Some he then sealed from exposure to air, others he left open. He then verified his hypotheses by observing the flasks for days. The open flasks rapidly developed contamination. The sealed flasks grew nothing. He then modified his experiment by opening the sealed flasks. They then became contaminated after exposure to air. Subsequently, he made swan-necked flasks. He would open these, at the distil tip of the curve, exposing the broth to air. No spoiling of the broth occurred. He surmised that the microscopic life forms, being particulate, could not traverse the curved neck of the flask; yet air still reached the broth. This experiment rebutted the claim that only air was needed to spoil the broth. The Null hypothesis would have been excluded (although not conceived at that time) in that the sealed flasks were universally sterile in contrast to the open ones. From this he developed his Law of Biogenesis: all life comes from life.

The Law of Biogenesis is a significant part of the verification process demonstrating evolution to be a false or rejected hypothesis/theory. For evolution to be true, spontaneous generation must be true and demonstrated. No experiment yet has shown it to occur. Evolution, as discussed later in this book, is actually a philosophic mindset or worldview/paradigm.

The History of Science
The history of science is a subject every Christian should be interested in, and be excited about for it abounds with the examples of God's greatness, power, his mercy, and divine plan for man. (The names of scientists who confessed faith in God or Jesus Christ are in bold type.)

In the earliest documented period of history (from the creation of the universe and world) we see that man had a complex social order and was able to reason, observe, and utilize his environment. In the first and second chapters of Genesis man was given the mantle of science by God. He was to: 1) classify the animals and 2) subdue and rule the earth - by implication to gain an understanding of its physical properties and use knowledge to develop technology. It also implied stewardship.

In the third chapter of Genesis after Adam and Eve sinned, God said, "Cursed is the ground because of you (Adam); in toil you shall eat of it all the days of your life ... by the sweat of your face you shall eat bread ... therefore the Lord God sent him out from the garden of Eden, to cultivate the ground from which he was taken." Thus, **Adam** learned to farm: sow and reap. In later chapters, but early in the history of man, the building of **Noah**'s ark is described. The technology for boat development (tools, pitch, structural integrity, units of measure, etc.) had to be known, and the dimensions given by God are similar to those of pre-World War I ocean liners, 450 feet long, 75 feet wide, 45 feet deep with a displacement of approximately 43,000 tons.

After the worldwide flood (considered to be 2000 BC by many creationists), the tower of Babel identifies early building technology using bricks, possibly a ziggurat. The initial chapters of Genesis also indicate record-keeping, for example, "'these are the generations of...'" may reflect separate recorded documents. The book of Job, considered a pre-Mosaic document, describes writing (Job 19:23-24). Bronze and copper use have been documented in excavations thought to be dated 2700 BC and 3000 BC respectively , from secular sources (yet are post-flood and thus are probably more recent in time). Thus man was utilizing science and its resultant technology from the earliest of times especially in the Fertile Crescent region of the world.

The early Egyptians developed a decimal system, a solar year, studied geometry, weaving, some medicinal arts (mummification, simple orthopedic techniques), incredible building technology, including possible levers and cantilevers, wheels, and pulleys to move stones.

The Babylonians developed a fixed unit of measure, multiplication tables, and study of the position of stars. This they mixed with mysticism to develop astrology.

The Bible and secular records chronicle that from the earliest times of man he has had innovative technology and complex societies. Yet, what we have in the archeological records must have occurred after the worldwide flood. They also reveal man to be sinful.

It should be noted that dating of the time periods by secular sources may be at variance with those determined by biblical references. This reflects that most methods are comparative, i.e. assign times by construction of the overlap and association of various past civilizations. As well, radiometric dating is not as useful as some propose because of its required assumptions which can create large variations. Thus, while one can often document the relative sequence of events fairly well, the absolute time periods are usually unknown.

600 BC to 200 BC

Considerable attention by secular historians is given to the Greek cultures in these times. Ionians, including Thales (624-546 BC) were committed to a naturalistic interpretation of the universe and were forerunners of the Atomists. They developed some elements of geometry, considered matter to be composed of four elements: earth, water, air, and fire. They perceived the sky as a dome, and the earth flat.

The Atomists were atheistic, materialists, and reduced all reality to atoms and void. They reasoned this, but did not have evidence for it. Democritus (460-360 BC), and Epicurus (342-270 BC) were its main advocates.

Pythagoras (530 BC) advanced geometry, and was motivated by the belief that the universe could be explained mathematically; in this he preempted Descartes (1600 AD).

Hippocrates (460-375 BC) developed an oath still considered appropriate today (except that some delete the portion where he refused to assist in abortion).

Aristotle (384-322 BC) had a profound impact on the world of science, for good and bad. The impact of his ideas was felt up until 1500-1600 AD. In part this was due to the support he received from Thomas Aquinas (1300 AD). Aristotle was primarily a philosopher who also observed nature. He developed the concept of reasoned deduction from a given premise, but did not emphasize verification.

He felt that function demands a form; each object trends towards its natural place. For example, he felt that heavy objects would fall faster to the earth than light ones because that was their proper place (this was repudiated by Galileo's experiments). He also accepted the Great Chain of Being, a form of evolutionary development of life, and that the earth was of the center of the universe. He did, however, produce a useful systematic catalog of living things.

In Archimedes (287-212 BC) the beginnings of the scientific method are seen. He would set forth a postulate and then conjecture what the result should be and test for it. He studied the concept of density, and the properties of the lever and pulley. Later Galileo would lean heavily upon his writings.

Euclid (325-270 BC) successfully summarized the learning of geometry in a textbook.

200 BC - 400 AD

Rome dominated the Mediterranean area for 1000 years. However, most of its scientific development was an extension of that developed by the Greeks, particularly Aristotle. Pliny (23-79 AD) produced an encyclopedia of nature, Lucretius propounded Atomism (that all life is composed of microscopic particles alone, i.e., no spiritual dimension). Celsus discussed surgical procedures and Galen (129-200) dissected animals, and made some initial observations on perfusion of blood within the body. Applied technology was probably Rome's greatest scientific achievement: public water and sewage systems, hospitals, and city planning (after the Greeks).

Ptolemy (100-170), in Egypt, propounded an earth-centered universe, named constellations, and performed early studies on light refraction.

St. Augustine (354-430) utilized Aristotelian ideas within a Christian context. The Greek Diophontus (200) developed algebraic equations.

With the fall of the Roman Empire, a chilling effect occurred in the European sciences for several hundred years, but it continued development in other parts of the world.

400- 1300 AD

Moslem states perpetuated Aristotle's, Euclid's, and Ptolemy's works during this time, translating the last two into the Almagest. Proclus in Turkey (410-485) wrote commentaries on Ptolemy and

Euclid. Isidor of Seville (560-636) wrote an encyclopedia of Greek learning. The Moslem chemist Geber (721-815 AD) prepared white lead, dyes, and varnishes. Rhazes (930) described small pox and measles, but accepted the Atomists' views. Omar Khayan (1048) improved astronomical tables and the Moslem calendar.

In the Byzantine Empire, Callinicus (620) developed "greek fire", a combination of petroleum, potassium nitrate, and quick lime which would burn on water and was used to repel the Arabic navy in 670 from Constantinople.

Learning did continue in European monastic communities as well. **Bede** (673-735) in England wrote about English history, portions of Pliny's writings, and astronomy in adjusting the calendar. He defended the earth as a sphere, tides as being affected by phases of the moon, and customized dating from the time of the birth of Christ. Monasteries continued to transcribe previous scientific works, and blended the writings of Plato and Aristotle into the Christian teachings. **Maimonides** (1135-1204), the prominent Jewish scholar, promoted Aristotelian science.

1300 - 1500 AD

Roger Bacon (1220-1292) reemphasized the need to experiment not just reason from observations; the last to do so was Archemides, 287 BC. He supported a round earth, constructed a magnifying glass, and discussed the use of gun powder.

Thomas Acquinas (1225-1274) supported Aristotle's concepts within a Catholic framework. He exalted human reason.

Johann Guttenberg (1398-1468) invented a printing press.

Jean Buridar (1300-1360) and **Nicole Oresome** (1382) anticipated some of Galileo's mechanical physics constructs. This supports recent research that the Dark Ages may not actually have been "dark" but that learning was largely confined to monasteries.

1500 - 1750 AD

This period is often cited as the onset of modern science, and the conflict between science and religion. However, the conflict was in reality between Aristotle's and Ptolemy's views (which the Catholic church had accepted) and the more refined mechanistic views of **Nicolas Copernicus** (1473-1543), **Galileo Galilei** (1564-1642), and others. Galileo affirmed a belief in God, but felt the church had misunderstood the scriptures. Interestingly, the measurements of planetary position available to Copernicus and Ptolemy supported either concept, an earth or sun centered solar system. N. Pearcey suggests Copernicus accepted the sun centered one for the philosophic reason that the sun symbolized God (a Christianized neo-Platonic view). This was also time when **Johannes Kepler** (1571-1630) believing in an intelligent, created universe, attempted to "think God's thoughts after Him" in understanding planetary movements. Thus, the scientific world was in a revolution of ideas regarding the universe. Unfortunately, some leaders of the Catholic church chose the incorrect side. Others however, even including the Pope, for a time, accepted the concepts of researchers like Galileo.

    Isaac Newton (1642-1727) probably the greatest scientist of all time, was a profound believer in the Christian God. He wrote commentaries on the book of Daniel and a history of Israel. He, like **Robert Boyle**, felt God intelligently designed the universe as a master engineer. Newton really pioneered physics, especially concepts regarding gravity, and the properties of light. Even with this he was only one of a host of scientists including **John Ray** (1627-1705) (biology), **Carolus Linnaeus** (1707-1778) (naturalist), **Boyle** (1627-1691) (chemist), **Francis Bacon** (1561-1626) (philosopher), **Blaise Pascal** (1623-1662) (math), **Kepler** (astronomy), **Nicolas Steno** (1638-1686) (geology), **Robert Hooke** (1635-1703) (biology), **Thomas Burnet** (1635-1715) (theologian/geology), and others who firmly set science on its present foundation. All believed that by studying nature they were learning about the character of God. (See **FIGURE 9**, "God Fearing Scientists.") This was in contrast to the Alchemists and Atomists who had no such assurance that the Universe they were studying was purposeful or orderly.

    While there was some tension between understanding the overlap and consistency between the divine revelation of scriptures and the observations of the physical environment, these men had great excitement in learning about the wonders of God's creation and His eternal plan. Unfortunately, secular men would utilize this tension in years to come to divide the two, with deleterious effects to both science and religion.

1750 - 1870 AD

    Bishop Butler's *Analogy of Religion* (1736) and **William Paley's** *Natural Theology* (early 1802) argued forcefully for a creator based universe worldview. But, from 1750 to 1870, the overthrow of this concept to that of a secular, atheistic one in science occurred. It was not because the evidence for a purely mechanical universe had become compelling, but rather as F. Hoyle, an evolutionist, has stated in 1983, "The evolutionary record leaks like a sieve ... There are so many flaws in Darwinism that one can wonder why it swept so completely through the scientific world, and why it is still endemic today." He answered, "Undoubtedly, however, the biggest thing going for Darwinism was that it broke the tyranny in which Christianity had held the minds of men for so many centuries." Many in western society wanted to be free from the moral restraints of Christianity.

The early geologists, **Nicolas Steno, John Woodward** (1665-1728)**, Thomas Burnet** (1635-1715)**, and Alexander Catcott** (1725-1779), did much service by establishing geology as a science. They advocated stratification by a watery deposition, fossils as being petrified remains of animals and plants, and accepted an age of the earth of approximately 4,000 - 6,000 years. They felt that all of this was consistent with Noah's flood. However, by the early 1800's, Hutton and Lyell were able, with essentially the same data, to sway others to the concept of a long age for the earth with strata being gradually built up under present processes, a process called uniformitarianism. It should be noted that then as now, present processes cannot explain the formation of much of the earth. In the Bridgewater treatise **William Buckland** (1784-1880), a professed Christian and flood geologist, gave way to support long age uniformitarian doctrine. By the mid-1800s the conversion from flood to uniform geology by professed Christians was complete as can be seen in the works of **Pye Smith** (1774-1851) and **Edward Hitchcock** (1793-1864). **Thomas Chalmers** (1780-1847), a theologian, popularized a large gap of time between Genesis 1:1 and 1:2. **Arnold Guyot** (1807-1884) expounded the idea that the creation days were to be correlated with fossil ages, concurrently being devised by **William Whewell** (1794-1866) and others. They organized the fossil record from simple to complex organisms. Thus **Guyot** felt each day was to be considered as millions of years. A variant of this was held by **Louis Agassiz** (1807-1873). He was a staunch opponent to evolution to the time of his death, and the premier naturalist of the mid-l800s. He believed that the earth had gone through repeated convulsions and recreations, a view similar to that held by **Georges Cuvier** (1769-1832), in the early 1800s.

Charles Bell (anatomy of the hand, 1774-1842), and **Richard Owen** (coined phrase for dinosaurs, 1804-1892), continued **Cuvier**'s development of anatomy and paleontology. In astronomy **William** (1738-1822)**, John** (1792-1871), and **Caroline** (1750-1848) **Herschel** with improved telescopes and lenses, diligently classified heavenly bodies, giving glory to God. In contrast, Laplace (1749-1827) denied the necessity of a creator in his Nebular Hypothesis.

The stage, philosophically, for a popular presentation of an Atomist, mechanistic universe was thus set by the time Darwin presented his *Origin of Species* in 1859. He simply made palatable what had already been propounded in the Great Chain of Being for hundreds of years. He suggested that by selective breeding pressure in nature (and practiced by men in the farming industry) life could gradually change from one type to another. He displayed the Galapagos Island Finches as evidence. However, all he showed was variation within a kind, yet by this he extrapolated to mean all living organisms from a common ancestor, that is, fish > reptiles > mammal > man. This has been called transmutation. He even admitted that he had no direct evidence for this, but stated that it would be found in the future. The evidence is still lacking until this day, according to many scientists.

While much of the effort of geology, biology, astronomy, and even anatomy were being directed towards what was to become the creation/evolution debate, other great and practical scientific discoveries were being made.

Improvements in measurements and weights as defined units were accepted so that various groups could compare results.

The development of thermodynamics was of imminent importance. Joseph Black (1728-1799) studied the characteristics of heat, e.g. the absorption of heat by substances as they went through solid to liquid phase. Benjamin Rumford (1753-1840) attempted to measure heat, but **James Joule** (1816-1889) successfully quantified it. Rudolph Clausius (1822-1888) developed the kinetic theory in 1857. Nicolas Carnot (1796-1832) measured the dissipation of energy from hot to cold bodies; important in the development of steam engines. **Andre Ampere** (1735-1836) measured the electrical current. Hans Oersted (1777-1751) studied the interplay of magnetism with electricity: the deflection of a compass needle when passed by current. **Michael Faraday** (1791-1867), who worked with **Humphrey Davy** (1778-1829), the chemist, discovered benzene, then went on to study electrolysis and electro-magnetism. **James Maxwell** (1831-1879) calculated magnetic lines of force. **Joseph Henry** (1797-1878) insulated electric wires, and constructed the first electric motor.

Exploration of uncharted regions of the earth was done by Friedrich Humboldt (1769-1859), and ocean currents were mapped by **Matthew Maury** (1806-1873). **John Dalton** (1766-1844) developed the Atomic Theory. Eli Whitney's cotton gin (1793) and George Stephanson's improved steam engine (1825) revolutionized commerce and travel. **Charles Babbage** (1792-1871) created a mechanical computer/calculator.

Medicine was advanced through the efforts of Edward Jenner (small pox vaccine, 1798); James Parkinson described the disease named after his name (1817) and Thomas Addison (1855) as well. **Joseph Lister** used phenol in surgical wounds (1867), Theophile Laennec developed a stethoscope (1890), Heinrich Schwab identified animal cells and studied metabolism as a chemical process of living organisms (1830), **Louis Pasteur** developed the Germ Theory (1865), and rejected the "Theory of Spontaneous Generation" (1860), and **Gregor Mendel** developed the foundations of genetics (1857).

1750 to 1870 was a great time of scientific discovery. Mankind has been greatly blessed by the discovery of electricity, electric motors, anesthesia, and anti-bacterial agents, steam engines, etc. Sadly though, it was a time in which atheistic man exalted himself: that he could control nature without God. Christian theologians and scientists were greatly vexed but largely overwhelmed by the voices of secular humanism. This of course led to the tragic concepts of eugenics by Herbert Spencer (1820-1903) and Francis Galton (1822-1911) (Darwin's cousin). Eugenics propounded that one people group or race was superior to another and thus they should enjoy certain advantages over the other. This led to its consequential outworking in international wars during the subsequent century.

When the writings of scientists who are Christians are viewed over time, a progressive trend is noted of extolling God in the midst of scientific discoveries (**Kepler**), winding down to acknowledgment of Him in the preface or conclusion (**Newton**) and finally no mention of Him in the work directly (**Pasteur**). The compartmentalization of science, religion, and philosophy as it pertains to Christianity became complete during the 1800s. Yet, the mechanistic, evolutionary religio-philosophic doctrines became acceptable and incorporated into scientific writings. It is as though scientists, as Christians, went underground. They were to remain largely so for the next 100 years.

1870 - Present

The foundational concepts discovered previously have successfully, for good or bad, been built upon in this century.

Dalton's "Atomic Theory" has been clarified by Friedrich Kekule (molecules combine in certain ratios, 1850), Vladimir Markonekov (carbon bonds, 1860), Max Planck (quantum mechanics late 1800s), Dmitri Mendeleev (atomic table, 1871), Marie Curie (isolation of uranium, 1898), Robert Millikian (charge of the electron, 1923), Ernst Rutherford (detection of alpha particles, and a theory of the nuclear atom, 1911) then improved by Niels Bohr (early 1900), Albert Einstein (special theory of relativity, and conversion of mass and energy which would lead to nuclear fission/fusion early 1900), Harold Urey (identification of deuterium, 1934), Ernst Lawrence, Leo Szilard, Edward Teller, Enrico Fermi, **Arthur Compton**, and Robert Oppenheimer (developed the first atomic bomb by fission, the release of energy by the splitting of atoms, 1945), and Marcus Oliphant (nuclear fission, 1934). Subatomic particle identification studies have been done by numerous people including Carl Anderson (1930s), and Robert Hofstadter (1960s).

Pasteur's Germ Theory was further developed by Robert Koch (isolation and growth of bacteria in an artificial media, 1876), Pierre Roux and Emil Behring (identification and production of antitoxin to diphtheria, late 1800s), Paul Ehrlich (staining of bacteria, isolation of antibodies to disease, and chemotherapeutic agents to syphilis, 1854-1915), **Ambrose Fleming** (identification of penicillin as a bactericidal agent, 1928). **Phillip Henry Gosse** (1810-1888) studied micromarine life forms.

Other medical advances include Edward Kendall (isolation of thyroxin, 1916), Hermann Muller (genetic mutations, and the effect of x-rays, early 1900s), Carl Cori (biochemical pathways, 1947), Linus Pauling (protein molecules, the abnormal structure of hemoglobinopathies, 1939), Fredrick Sanger (isolation and amino acid sequencing of insulin, 1953), and John Eccles (chemical alteration of neural synapses, 1963).

Further subcellular studies were done by Wendell Stanley (isolation of viruses, and the study of their properties, 1933), Heinz Frankel-Conrat (isolation of nucleic acids, 1955), Peter Medawar (tissue transplantation, 1960), Francis Crick and James Watson (structure of DNA, 1953), and Arthur Kornberg (synthetic DNA molecule, 1956), **Francis Collins** (led a team to sequence the human genome). Many other studies regarding the chemical properties of living organisms have been done. To record them would require many more pages.

Technological developments included **Alexander Bell** (telephone), Thomas Edison (phonograph, light bulb, motion picture, 1300 patents), Ferdinand Zeppelin (balloon aircraft), Rudolf Diesel (diesel engine), Alfred Nobel (dynamite), **William Ramsey** and **Fredric Kenyon** (archeology), **Orville and Wilbur Wright** (flight), **George Carver** (agricultural science) and Bill Gates (computer programming). **Michael Pupin** (early 1900s) advanced the technologic use of x-ray in medicine.

During this time numerous scientists have continued to advance a mechanistic, atheistic view of life in the universe, from Stanley Miller (organic molecules), Theodosius Dobszanky (transmutation by gradual mutational change), or R. Goldschmidt (transmutation by massive rapid mutational change), W. Alvarez (multiple geologic catastrophes), Richard Leakey (ape to man evolution), to James Jean and George Gamow (expanding, long age universe). At the same time, the liberty to express faith in God was hampered and even shunned. Thus, many of the scientists of this time period were probably believers in God, yet were unwilling to express their faith for fear of persecution. One survey (which was done confidentially) did reveal that a belief in God was common among the scientists surveyed.

A spattering of Christians from the late 1800s to early/mid 1900s challenged the evolutionary doctrines. **J. W. Dawson** and **J. D. Dana** (geology) supported day/age creationism. **G. F. Wright** (theology/geology) reverted from Darwinism to creationism. **George McCready Price** in 1923 wrote a popular flood geology text. **B. Nelson** and **B. O'Toole** (theology) exposed evolutionary assumptions especially in the areas of biology. In the 1930s **Sir J.**

Ambrose Fleming, D. Dewar, and B. Acworth formed the Evolution Protest Movement. The Christian scientists Georges Lemaitre and Arthur Eddington supported "big bang" theories.

In recent years, in opposition to many of the scientific community, a few scientists have successfully challenged the assumptions underlying evolution. These have included such men as W. Lammerts (botany), Henry and John Morris (hydrology/geology), A. Snelling and S. Austin (geology), J. Baumgardner (astrophysics, whose sophisticated computer program can describe flood or uniformitarian deposition depending on the preset assumptions placed in the program), R. Humphries, T. Barnes, and L. Vardiman (physics), R. Gentry and D. Gish (chemistry), among others. A. E. Wilder-Smith (chemist), and K. Ham (teacher) have been successful in addressing the implications of evolution. While these are trained scientists and teachers, their writings reflect a significant concern on the influx and perpetration of non-Christian religio-philosophic views into the realm of science. The present successful, scientific method developed out of a Christian worldview. If secular scientists continue to reject these foundations we may see an increasing devolution of science. This is already apparent in the writings of some. For example, there are well known secular scientists who support the Gaia paradigm that the earth is a living organism, and mystic physics in which reality is rejected; or reincarnation like Carl Sagan, who blended his planetary research with his eastern mystic views.

Yet science, the study of our physical surroundings, if rightly understood helps man and glorifies God.

Conclusion

Science is a study of our physical environment. It is a God-given attribute of man. In the book of Genesis, God commanded Adam to name the animals, and rule the earth. In this command we see the two attributes of scientific study: 1) observation and classification of matter, and 2) observation and manipulation of the physical properties of matter. Technology is developed from this. Science cannot answer questions of worth, beauty, or ultimate cause/purpose.

Our physical universe is not as God originally made it. While it reveals His divine power and attributes to us (Romans 1) it is no longer only good; for "all of creation groans, waiting for its redemption", (Romans 8:22). Thus, questions of "why would God allow this", often must be answered "because of man's free will and his choice of sin this occurred." "Acts of God" are only such because of His allowing of man's sin to affect the physical universe. Only by the study of God's word, the Bible, can we begin to understand what is and is not His will, and the effects of sin on the creation.

Men have, since Adam's sin, chosen to believe in God or not. Once the decision is made a person follows one of two world views; a materialistic, atheistic one or a creator-based one. The impact is profound (see philosophy). While the church has been accused of opposing the advancement of science, this has usually occurred when it accepted certain secular concepts such as a flat earth or the earth at the center of the solar system; and then it attempted to apply this to incorrectly understood tenets of Christianity. Yet, atheistic views have led to a severe misuse of science. Evolutionary based eugenics has had a profound effect in recent times of war and Imperial expansion. It has led to unnecessary medical concepts and procedures, the misguided use of millions/billions of dollars in certain kinds of space and geologic research and anthropologic and biologic research.

God-fearing scientists played a major role in the development of the scientific method. Thus, the Christian should enjoy science, but he or she should test the philosophic bent behind its presentation. Truth does "spring from the earth", and "the heavens do declare the glory of God". A correct understanding of scientific observations should be and is consistent with a correct understanding of spiritual and philosophic principles.

FIGURE 9

God Fearing Scientists (partial list)

	Century						
	14th	15th	16th	17th	18th	19th	20th-21st
Biology				Ray	Linnaeus	Pasteur, Fabre Cuvier, Mendel Owen, Gosse Gosse	Colins Dewar Nelson
Chemistry				Boyle		Kelvin Davy, Dalton	Wilder-Smith Stine, Carver
Astronomy			Copernicus	Kepler, Galileo		Herschel	Maunder
Physics/Math		Buridar Oresome	DaVinci	Newton Pascal, Huygens Harris	Whiston Henry	Babbage, Joule Morse, Raleigh Henry, Flemming Maxwell, Faraday Stokes, Riemann	von Braun Humphries
Medicine				Harvey		Lister, Bell Simpson, Rush Virchow, McDowell	Kelly, Carrel
Exploration, Paleontology Oceanography, Geology Philosophy, Archeology		Columbus Magellan	Bacon	Steno Burnet	Woodward Dwight Catcott	Livingstone Maury, Agassiz Buckland	Sayce, Ramsay Irwin, White Duke, Morris Snelling
Religion	Wycliff		Tyndale, Luther Calvin		Wesley, Edwards Butler	Chalmers	O'Toole Ryrie

CHAPTER 5

CONCLUSION:
THE INTERFACING OF RELIGION, PHILOSOPHY, AND SCIENCE IN DEVELOPING A TRANSFORMING CHRISTIAN WORLDVIEW

The Triune Nature of Man

As has been discussed throughout this book, the primary purpose of man's existence is to glorify God and have fellowship with Him. Jesus said, "And this is eternal life, that they may know Thee, the only true God, and Jesus Christ whom thou hast sent" (John 17: 3).

God created man as a triune being: spirit, soul, and body. In Hebrews 4:12 it says, "For the word of God is living and active and sharper than any two-edged sword, and piercing as far as the division of soul and spirit, of both joints and marrow, and able to judge the thoughts and intentions of the heart." In another place Paul stated, "Do you not know that you are the temple of God and God's Spirit dwells in you." (1 Corinthians 3:16) Even Jesus said to the Jews, "'Destroy this temple, and in three days I will raise it up.' The Jews therefore said, 'It took forty-six years to build this temple, and will You raise it up in three days?' But He was speaking of the temple of His body." (John 2:19-21) Our bodies are also referred to as tabernacles in 2 Corinthians 5:4, "For indeed while we are in this tent (tabernacle), we groan, being burdened…" (See **Figure 10**).

God uses three areas of our existence to reveal Himself to us, and these intersect at every level of our being - Spirit, Soul, and Body (flesh). These levels correspond to the realms of Religion, Philosophy, and Science. With science one can observe and interact with the physical nature of the matter. It is assessed through five senses, the properties of it can be studied and technology developed from it. It gives us an awareness of God's power and creativity. The spiritual realm can impact it as when a supernatural healing occurs through prayer. The philosophic or realm of the mind overlaps it as reasoning is required for assessment of the properties of physical matter. However, the value of something is based entirely in philosophy and religion, and scientific endeavor can never address this yet it provides the physical data upon which worth is determined. Issues of the ultimate beginning or ending are based entirely in religion but some overlap occurs with philosophy and science through extrapolation of the observed universe. Thus each realm of our existence is separate and it is also unified in that each part overlaps the other parts. (See **Figure 11,** "Three Ways of Knowing Reality", and **Figure 12,** "The Interfacing of Religion, Philosophy, and Science".)

Because of Adam's initial sin, all of mankind has experienced corruption at every level of existence. This is true of the Creation as well (Romans 8:20, 21). Thus religion, philosophy, and science are defective. To communicate with sinful man, God who is holy had to re-establish a knowledge of Himself to man in the earth. He did this by the general revelation of truth given by His Spirit through an awareness of the Creation, and then more specifically through selected individuals over a 1600 year period. Finally, He revealed the exact character of His essence in the God/man Jesus Christ- who spoke on many things including those already recorded prophesies regarding Himself. These writings have been compiled into the Bible. The basic concepts of His message have never changed; the Holy Scriptures are internally consistent, and accurate historically.

Religion

Religion should make man aware of the spiritual dimension. While it is real, it cannot be measured physically; though the spirit realm can impact the physical and emotional arenas. As well, the spirit can be "oppressed or suppressed" by the soul and flesh. Miracles, by definition, occur through a superceding of natural principles by spiritual ones. Regardless of the opposition to the concept of the spirit it remains a valid concept. Many things remain outside of the physical and philosophical domains and greatly impact mankind. To ignore this is to be ignorant. (Those who by a naturalistic philosophy exclude the spirit realm do so by combining their philosophy and religion together. And yet, they are utterly unable to demonstrate a proof of its non-existence.)

Philosophy

God uses the methods of philosophy to give understanding and wisdom to mankind. He says, "Come now, let us reason together," (Isaiah 1:18). Yet, philosophers like David Hume argued against the logic of cause and effect; and thus against the concept of a Creator and Creation. To them personal perception was the only reality (which of course is simply a choice of self aggrandizement). Yet, taken to its obvious conclusion, all reality would become absurd. The issues of life require that certain *a priori* assumptions must be made: there is a physical reality, it has common reproducible phenomena, and each man (without disability) can experience them through the senses. The logical corollary is that as we design, make or mold objects out of the physical creation there must be one who made us. However, even though we are part of the creation, it does not necessitate that the one who made us must be contained within it. (And in fact this is specifically addressed in the Biblical scriptures.) This view was propounded by Paley in the 1800's and remains a valid assumption.

Science

God has and does use science to reveal His divine attributes and power to man. It is by His mind that we are even able to practice science. Men who study science, and deny God, must purposefully and diligently reject the obvious revelation of God in nature. The only other option than a Creator is spontaneous generation (self-organizing matter) and transmutational change (fish to bird etc.) development of all life from non-life. Scientific observations have never directly supported these concepts. (See "Why I Believe in God and not Evolution".) Researchers who adhere to these concepts have a true "blind faith" and "suppress the truth in unrighteousness" (Romans 1:18). The scientist and anyone else who accurately observes nature recognizes that incredible complexity and design argues for a designer. Science was born out of a belief in a benevolent Creator. In observing the properties of nature and developing technology from these observations, man is fulfilling God's command to "subdue the earth". This command is God-given even if some individual men have distorted the use of science. Each will have to account for his actions before the Judge of all. The technologic comforts of today are the fruit of the faith of those early scientists (see Chapter 4 Science).

Overlapping of these Realms of Existence

To understand the "truth" of reality requires God's Spirit, for no man has a full understanding of things. (In fact man has very little understanding.) Only God can put things in perspective. To know truth one must assume God will teach him. God has promised this by three vehicles: understanding of the Creation, His Word (the Bible), and the revelation of His Spirit. (See **FIGURES 10-12.**) These three will never contradict each other. By these man can come to a correct perspective of life.

The Bible makes an interesting association between the soul and the spirit. John 4:24 says, "God is Spirit, and those who worship Him must worship in spirit and truth." Reckoning God worthy of our praise (worshipping) is an act of both the mind and the spirit, and can be manifested in the flesh (e.g. the raising of hands etc.). There have been many religious movements throughout history which have attempted to worship God but they did not and do not have truth or His Spirit. Some have denied the Creator yet desired spiritual experiences (e.g. New Age Movement). Others have denied the existence of Hell (e.g. Jehovah's Witnesses). A few have told mankind that each is a god (e.g. Mormonism). These religions err in their knowledge of the truth. They may be "spiritual" and worship a spirit, but it is not God's Holy Spirit.

Salvation

The Bible teaches that at the time a person accepts Jesus Christ's atonement for sins, His death and resurrection, and chooses to obey God, his spirit becomes completely regenerated, and empowered by God's Spirit (see Jesus interaction with Nicodemus, John 3:1-10). As such he is a child of God and a partaker of His divine nature (Romans 8:10-16; 2 Peter 1:3, 4). Having been "born again" every Christian is then to be formed into the image of Christ. Each is to "put on Christ." The trial of each is the war between the "flesh" (defined as the body and soul in the Bible) and the spirit (Galatians 3). That is, before a person was born again the spirit yielded to the impulses and reasoning of the "flesh", for the entire being was corrupted. But, after being "born again", a man's spirit is no longer corrupted, yet the flesh (soul and body) still is.

The Christian struggles within (Romans 7, 8). The only way out of this difficulty is to renew the mind to God's word, deny the ungodly bodily impulses, and yield to the direction of God's Spirit. The maturing Christian must become spirit rather soul dominated. Each believer needs to allow God to renovate his/her entire being. He does much of this by working through the realms of religion, philosophy, and science. While the process can be painful, at times, the fruit is eternal righteousness (right conduct and relationship with God), peace (no condemnation and a knowledge of God's love), and joy (knowing the person has an eternal existence with a loving Father/Creator and others) (see Hebrews 12:11 and Romans 14:17). The Christian is then able to accurately defend the Faith, "always ready to make a defense to everyone who asks you to give an account for the hope that is in you, yet with gentleness and reverence" (1 Peter 3:15).

FIGURE 10

God's Tabernacle

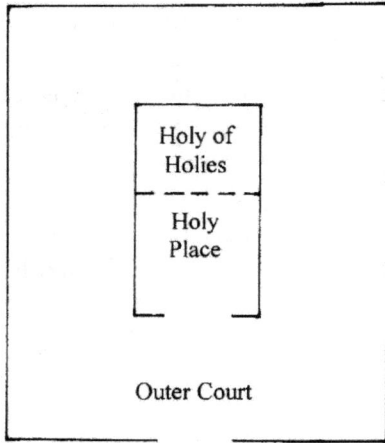

The Tabernacle of Man

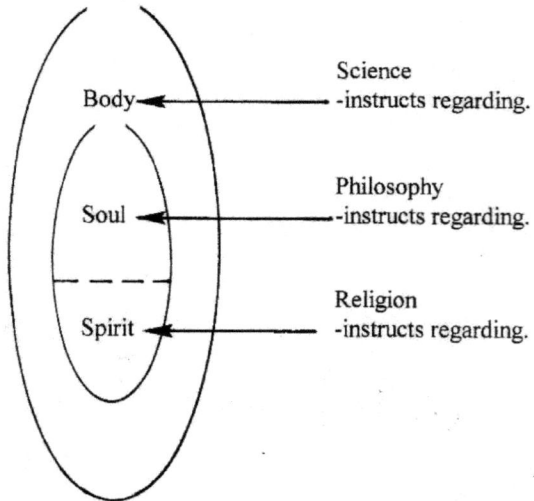

FIGURE 11

Three Ways of Knowing Reality

1. **Observation of nature (science)**
   - assessed by 5 senses
   - technology developed from it
   - gives knowledge of God's work
     including the functions of the
     human body

   Psalm 85:11; 19:1

2. **Reason (philosophy)**
   - evaluated through mind
   - deals with aspects or morals, conduct, identity
   - used to understand God
   - interface between spirit and flesh
   - influences the will

   2 Tim. 2:15; Col. 2:8

3. **Revelation (religion)**
   - received by our spirit from God's Spirit
   - reveals ultimate purposes
   - by it we have fellowship with God
   - motivates conduct
   - communion with God's Spirit

   John 4:23

FIGURE 12

The Interfacing of Religion, Science and Philosophy

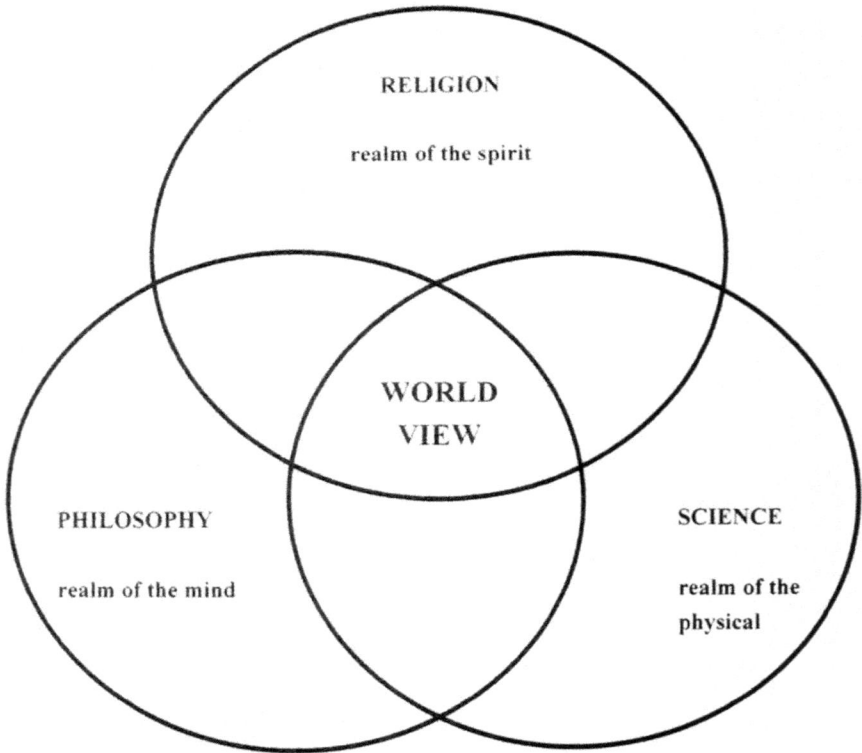

RELIGION

realm of the spirit

WORLD
VIEW

PHILOSOPHY

realm of the mind

SCIENCE

realm of the
physical

WHAT MUST I DO TO BE SAVED?

Ancient writings and all cultures of the world teach about the Creator, a worldwide flood which destroyed the surface of the earth because of the sins of man, and the need of a blood sacrifice to atone for those and the continuing sins of man to be at peace with Almighty God.

The sacred scriptures of the **Bible** teach that as a man **Jesus Christ** came from God, to die as the blood payment for all men's sins, and that whoever accepts His sacrifice for their sins will be forgiven of them. As God, **Christ Jesus** can then give them new life, by recreating the hearts (within their spirit by the power of God's Holy Spirit) of those forgiven. They can then, grow in the grace and knowledge of God the Father, and live eternally with Him now and after death.

Would you like to do this? If so, the **AACTS** steps are suggested:
1) Romans 3:23 (NASB) says, "For all have sinned (disobeyed) and come short of the glory of God." **Admit** that you have sinned.
2) Romans 6:23 states, "For the wages of sin is death, but the gift of God is eternal life through Jesus Christ our Lord." **Acknowledge** that sin is leading you to death (physically, emotionally, and spiritually).
3) Romans 10:9-10 says "that if you confess with your mouth Jesus as Lord, and believe in your heart that God raised Him from the dead, you will be saved; for with the heart a person believes, resulting in righteousness" (right standing with God) "and with the mouth he confesses, resulting in salvation," (freed forever from the punishment of sin). If you **Confess** the **Teachings** of the Bible, that Jesus is Lord and He died for your sins, you will experience **Salvation**.
4) So **AACTS** now! And get involved in a local church that teaches the Bible.

WHY I BELIEVE IN GOD
AND NOT EVOLUTION

I believe there are strict scientific, philosophical, and religious reasons to not adhere to evolution.

Design evokes a designer/creator. Nature and the observations of science support this concept. There are definable, reproducible phenomenon in nature (e.g. the law of gravity). Common design principles are seen among various life forms, e.g. light receptor systems, smell, locomotion, energy transformation, waste production, flight, and others. A common genetic code contains these details. Analogy has been made of the factory with the functions of the cell. The eye is compared to the camera, the digestive system with a fuel burning engine, eighth cranial nerve vestibular function with that of a gyroscope, etc. Nature abounds and attests of common design features both within the organic and inorganic world. Man only utilizes design features already present in the natural world.

Contrary to what some scientists believe, there is little evidence to support a non-designed, mechanistic development (evolution) of life from non-life. Numerous studies have shown that life could not have developed from simple organic molecules on our present earth. Some have devised convoluted arguments as to how life began on another planet and was somehow transferred here (via comet, etc.), yet absolutely no substantial evidence exists for organic extraterrestrial life.

The concept of natural or artificial selection does not support evolution or transmutation from simple to complex life forms. It is even questionable whether there is such a thing as a simple life form. Regardless, many evolutionists believe that the mechanism of selective pressure on mutational alterations has resulted in this supposed progression. In contradiction, enhancing the mutation rates among bacteria and fruit flies have done much to help in the understanding of individual gene function, but has scant effect in changing fruit flies or bacteria into other organisms. In fact, just the opposite occurs. A fly with double the set of wings can't fly whereas the normal one can. An antenna in place of the eye is debilitating. Bacteria loose adaptive properties. The concept of gene mutational load and the necessity of DNA repair mechanisms argue against the usefulness of mutations. Natural selection does occur however. Debilitated animals are removed from the herd by predators, or die from organic diseases. But this serves to preserve or even cleanse the gene pool from some of the effects of mutations. Thus, there is little empirical evidence that it forms the basis of trans-mutational (i.e. reptile to bird) change. In addition, most so-called vestigial organs have been shown to have a functional purpose as knowledge has advanced, e.g. tonsils.

Some will say that the fossil record reveals the evidence for transmutation. Yet, certain non-empirical and preconceived ideas must be accepted concerning the record. I, for one, do not accept that the record was the product of slow accumulation of layer upon layer of sedimentary soil, with life forms occasionally trapped in it. There is much evidence for catastrophic deposition. Present conditions do not support the wide scale preservation of whole large animals by simply dying and settling in the ooze. Yet, catastrophic preservation of intact animals and humans has been shown at Pompeii. However, because animal and plant life lie together in a given strata, it does not follow that they necessarily lived together; but only that they may have been buried together. Even when one accepts some sort of slow progressive sedimentary buildup, there is not gradual transition from one life form to another. Because of this, and the absolute commitment to trans-mutational change, some have devised the concept of punctuated equilibrium, which surmises that the transition occurred rapidly in small numbers not allowing for preservation of sufficient numbers of organisms. Thus, it is a non-verifiable idea to explain why there is no evidence for transitional life forms. Using this concept some have propounded upward, sideward, and downward evolution. It may be a philosophy or paradigm, but it is not a working hypothesis, because it cannot be tested for falsity.

One might ask why when the observations of science cry out for design and a designer, do some scientists cling to a mechanistic (non-purposeful, non-designed) view of the universe. The reasons are probably as varied as the individuals involved. Some choose to believe in evolution because it allows them to dictate their own views of right and wrong. Unfortunately when whole societies have believed this it has led to anarchy. The so called battle between science and religion is really a battle of world views: the mechanistic view of life verses a creation view of life. Nonetheless, I do believe the concepts and observations of science better support design and thus a designer/creator.

For the above reasons and many others, I believe in God and not evolution.

Sincerely,

John G. Leslie PhD, MD, PhD

SELECTED BIBLIOGRAPHY
(Christian and Secular)

Introduction
1. Michael Medved. Hollywood vs. America (New York NY: Harper Collins, 1992).

Chapter 1
2. Watchman Nee. The Spiritual Man (New York NY: Christian Fellowship Publishers, 1977).
3. Paul F. Kiene. The Tabernacle of God in the Wilderness of Sinai (Grand Rapids MI: Zondervan, 1977).
4. Charles Ryrie. The Ryrie Study Bible (Chicago IL: Moody Press, 1978).
5. Clarence Larkin. The Greatest Book on Dispensational Truth in the World (Philadelphia PA: Rev. Clarence Larkin Est., 1920).

Chapter 2
6. The Publications of the American Tract Society, Volume 8 (New York NY: American Tract Society, 1830).
7. R. Laird Harris, Gleason L. Archer Jr., Bruce K. Waltke. Theological Wordbook of the Old Testament (Chicago IL: Moody Bible Institute, 1980).
8. World Book Encyclopedia, Volume R (Chicago IL: World Book Inc., 1995).
9. James Strong. Strong's Concordance (Nashville TN: Abingdon Press, 1974).
10. Henry Morris. The Long War Against God (Grand Rapids MI: Baker Book House, 1989).
11. David Noebel. Understanding the Times (Eugene OR: Harvest House Publishers, 1995).
12. Dave Breese. Seven Men Who Rule the World from the Grave (Chicago IL: Moody Press, 1990).

13. W. S. Sahakian. <u>History of Philosophy</u> (New York NY: Barnes and Noble, 1968).
14. Walter Martin. <u>The Kingdom of the Cults</u> (Minneapolis MN: Bethany Fellowship, Inc., 1972).
15. Walter Martin. <u>The New Cults</u> (Santa Ana CA: Vision House, 1980).
16. Katrina Marti. <u>Making the Journey from Mormonism to Biblical Christianity</u> (Phoenix AZ: Aimazing Publishing and Marcom, 2012).
17. J. Ankerberg and John Weldon. <u>The Anker Series on: The New Age Movement, Jehovah's Witnesses, The Masonic Lodge, The Occult, The Mind Sciences, Spirit Guides, False Views About Jesus, and Psychic Readings</u> (Eugene OR: Harvest House Publishers, 1987-97).
18. John Warwick Montgomery. <u>History and Christianity</u> (Downers Grove IL: Intervarsity Press, 1965).
19. <u>AntiNicean Fathers in The Christian Library CD</u> (Albany OR: AGES Digital Library, 1997).
20. Clyde Cluckholn and Dorothea Leighton. <u>The Navajo</u> (Cambridge MA: Harvard University Press, 1974).
21. Craig Stephen Smith. <u>Whiteman's Gospel</u> (Winnipeg Manitoba: Indian Life Books, 1997).
22. <u>William Carey in Glimpses – The Serampore Compact, Issue 109</u> (Worcester PA: Christian History Institute, 1999).
23. Alfred Guillaume. <u>Islam</u> (Harmondsworth GB: Penguin Books, 1954.
24. Henry M. Morris. "Creation, Christians, and the Quran" in <u>Back to Genesis</u> (El Cajon CA: Institute for Creation Research, 1998).
25. David Ben-Gurion. <u>The Jews in Their Land</u> (Garden City NY: Doubleday & Co., 1974).
26. Derek Prince. <u>Three Messages for Israel</u> (Ft. Lauderdale FL: Derek Prince Publications, 1969).
27. Clifford A. Wilson. <u>Rocks, Relics, and Biblical Reliability</u> (Grand Rapid MI: Zondervan, 1977).
28. Joseph P. Free. <u>Archeology and the Bible</u> (Wheaton IL: Scripture Press Publications, 1974).
29. Don Richardson. <u>Eternity in Their Hearts</u> (Ventura CA: Regal Books, 1984).

Chapter 3

30. Will Durant. The Story of Philosophy (Garden City NY: Garden City Publishing Co. Inc., 1927).
31. Francis A. Schaeffer. Escape from Reason (Downers Grove IL: Intervarsity Press, 1972).
32. Francis A. Schaeffer. How Should We Then Live? (Westchester IL: Crossway Books, 1976).
33. Anthony Flew. A Dictionary of Philosophy (New York NY: St. Martins Press, 1947).
34. M. Guizot. Meditations on the Actual State of Christianity (London GB: John Murray, 1866).
35. Julian Huxley. Evolution in Action (New York NY: Mentor Books, 1957).
36. Charles Darwin. The Origin of the Species (New York NY: Merrill and Baker, reprint of the sixth edition, 1872).
37. Fred Hoyle and C. Wickramsinghe. Evolution from Space (London GB: Granada, 1983).
38. George Grant. The Legacy of Planned Parenthood (Brentwood TN: Wolgemuth and Hyatt, 1988).
39. Phillip E. Johnson. Reason in the Balance (Downers Grove IL: Intervarsity Press, 1995).
40. Charles E. Rice. 50 Questions on the Natural Law (San Francisco CA: Ignatius Press, 1993).
41. Peter Singer. Practical Ethics (Cambridge: Cambridge University Press, 1980).
42. Etienne Gilson. God and Philosophy (New Haven CT: Yale University Press, 1963).
43. Bishop Joseph Butler. Analogy of Religion, Natural and Revealed, to the Constitution and Course of Nature (New York NY: Harper and Brothers, 1854).
44. Hilaire Belloc. The Crisis of Civilization (New York NY: Fordham Press, 1937).

Chapter 4

45. James B. Conant. On Understanding Science (New York NY: Mentor Books, 1995).
46. William Grange Clarke. An Investigation into the Nature and Structure of Science as it Affects Christian Apologetics

(Partial fulfillment for Master of Arts from William Carey International University, 1984).

47. Thomas S. Kuhn. <u>The Structure of Scientific Revolutions, Volume 2</u> (Chicago IL: University of Chicago Press, 1970).

48. John G. Kemeny. <u>A Philosopher Looks at Science</u> (Princeton NJ: D. Van Nostrand Co., 1970).

49. William C. Dampier. <u>A Shorter History of Science</u> (Cambridge: University Press, 1944).

50. Henry M. Morris. <u>Men of Science Men of God</u> (San Diego CA: Creation-Life Publishers, 1982).

51. Dan Graves. <u>Scientists of Faith</u> (Grand Rapids MI: Kregel Resources, 1996).

52. Nancy R. Pearcey and Charles B. Thaxton. <u>The Soul of Science, Christian Faith, and Natural Philosophy</u> (Wheaton IL: Crossway Books, 1994).

53. Arnold Guyot. <u>Creation</u> (New York NY: Charles Scribner's Sons, 1889).

54. Henry M. Morris. <u>The Genesis Flood</u> (Grand Rapids MI: Baker Book House, 1981).

55. Ken Ham. <u>The Lie</u> (El Cajon CA: Creation-Life Publishers, 1987).

56. Ronald L. Numbers. <u>The Creationists</u> (New York NY: Alfred A. Knopf, 1992).

ABOUT THE AUTHOR

Dr. John G. Leslie graduated with a BS from American University, Washington, DC (1973), a Ph D. in Experimental Pathology from the University of Utah School of Medicine (1980), a Doctorate of Medicine at Oral Roberts University (1989) and Residency in Internal Medicine/Pediatrics from the University of Oklahoma - Tulsa Branch (1993). He has been Board Certified in Pediatrics and Internal Medicine. He also has a Bible School Certificate of Completion from the Word of Faith Bible College, Dallas, Texas (1982), and a PhD in Archaeology and Biblical History, Trinity Southwest University, Albuquerque (2012).

Dr. Leslie has worked with several leading scientists both in the United States and abroad. He has been an author in publications such as The New England Journal of Medicine, Biochemical and Biophysical Research Communications, Connective Tissue Research, and others including foreign journals. He has written communications in several newspapers including the American Medical Association News, and The American Academy of Pediatric News. Articles have appeared in Ex Nihilo and in its Technical Journal issues.

He is or has been a member of the West Coast Connective Tissue Society (USA), Australian-New Zealand Connective Tissue Society, American Medical Association, Tulsa Medical Society, New Mexico Medical Society, Christian Medical Society, Pro Life Victoria (Australia), Creation Research Society, Oklahomans for Life, New Mexico Right to Life, American Academy for Medical Ethics, and the Phi Theta Kappa Honor Society. He has been awarded a Ewing Foundation Student Fellowship (1987) for oncology research, and he was an Eagle Scout in the Boy Scouts of America.

His early work involved protein structure and function studies. He then pursued studies in protein metabolism. Further studies included the development of monoclonal antibodies to various biologically active proteins. More recently, he investigated the structure of DNA in certain cancers. At present, he works as a physician and participates in an annual archaeological dig in Jordan.

You can visit the author's website at
www.DefendingTheChristianFaith.org

www.ingramcontent.com/pod-product-compliance
Lightning Source LLC
Chambersburg PA
CBHW060524030426

42337CB00015B/1991